FORWARD
STOP
REVERSE

*Adapted from a manuscript by Katherine Whaley.

This book is dedicated the the great Kim Thompson. It has been a real privilege to work with him over the years. The contribution he has made to this exciting popular art form has been extraordinary.

Editor: Kim Thompson | Book Design: Kim Deitch | Production: Paul Baresh & Emory Liu | Deskman: Jason T. Miles | Associate Publisher: Eric Reynolds | Publishers: Gary Groth & Kim Thompson | FANTAGRAPHICS BOOKS, INC. Seattle, Washington, USA | *The Amazing, Enlightening and Absolutely True Adventures of Katherine Whaley* is copyright © 2013 Kim Deitch. | This edition is copyright © 2013 Fantagraphics Books, Inc. | Permission to reproduce content must be obtained from the author or publisher. | ISBN 978-1-60699-631-7 | First printing: May, 2013 | Printed in Hong Kong

1987
?
HEY ELLIE! LOOK!

GOSH! What is it?
Don't know. Looks like some kind of movie machine!

There's the switch!

NUTS! It doesn't work!

WAIT! Here's a plug!

THE MACHINE WHIRLS INTO LOUD, RATCHETY ACTIVITY AS THE SCREEN LIGHTS UP, SHOWING AN AMAZING, VIVID, MOVING PICTURE!
WOW!
Look at THAT!

Yeah!
She's beautiful!

The Kids watch as the strange scene plays out.

YIKES!
THEN SUDDENLY THE SCENE IS ENVELOPED IN A BURST OF BRIGHT YELLOW FIRE!

THE ODD MACHINE HAS BURST INTO FLAME!

WHAT IN CREATION!

COVERING THE FLAMING MACHINE WITH A CANVAS SHEET, SHE MANAGES TO SMOTHER THE BLAZE!
OH MY LORD!

SOON...
LOADING
TODAY
TODAY
LUCKY FOR YOU YOUR FOLKS AREN'T HERE!
WHEN THEY HEAR ABOUT THIS, YOU'LL CATCH IT FOR SURE!

HOTEL
Tell you what. I'll make a deal with you.

HOTEL
I won't tell your folks about this,
but you two better stay upstairs with me where I can keep an eye on you!
Thanks Aunt Kate, you're a pal!

There, now. If you're so set on seeing movies, you can watch them right here on TV while I do my knitting.
Yes Ma'm!

But soon Kate drifts off to sleep.
And Ellie is snooping again.
SO MANY INTERESTING THINGS!

?
Like that odd wooden head up on a shelf over Aunt Kate's desk.

Then she notices an old framed photo on Kate's desk.

HEY! She looks just like the pretty woman in the movie that burned up!
GOSH! Was that Aunt Kate?

Perhaps a better question might be, just who IS Aunt Kate?
But, on some level, Katherine Whaley seems to have heard this child and her unconscious mind ruminates on strange memories of days gone by!
WILD!
WEIRD!
SEEMINGLY IMPROBABLE DAYS!

....And yet strangely true, too, for these are the events that inform and illuminate...
ROBESPIERRE
Let There Be Enlightenment

The Amazing, Enlightening And Absolutely True
THE MARCH OF HUMANITY
In six stages
Today's man is between stage 5 and 6.
Today's woman is at stage 6
1
2
3
4
5
6
Women lead the way.

Adventures of Katherine Whaley!

To tell you the truth, I was a little surprised when I got the package and long letter from Eleanor Whaley last year. I hadn't heard from her for a while and I was beginning to think she was mad at me. While I'd technically honored our agreement to tell her story, in a recent book of mine, exactly as she'd told it to me, I did take some liberties editing and illustrating it and her silence, after I'd sent her copies, struck me as kind of ominous.

In it,* I told the story of how Ellie and her brother, Sid, found and rescued their Uncle Gar, thought to be dead, and made a fortune in rare, collectible bottle caps in the bargain.

Out of Ellie's portion of the money they made, she and her husband, Warren, built a house in upstate New York on a piece of land that runs along the Chemung river about fifteen miles from the city of Elmira.

I interviewed Ellie there for the story we did together a few years ago. At the time, Warren was in Iraq serving with the American army and Ellie was living in the house they built along with her brother, Sid, her Uncle Gar, and an old red macaw named Noodles.

I hadn't really gotten a good look at the property when I made my earlier visits, but *did* notice various old, run-down buildings on it. Ellie told me the property had been left to her by an Aunt and that she and Warren were eventually planning to clear the land and try their luck at some sort of farming.

* "The Sunshine Girl," in *Deitch's Pictorama*, 2008, Fantagraphics

Here is a portion of Ellie's letter. "Hi Kim. I'm sorry to have been such a stranger, but I got a really bad piece of news just a week before your book got here about my husband Warren. He was killed in a roadside bombing in Iraq and it hit me really hard. To be honest, I was kind of surprised at *how* hard. I didn't really tell you very much about Warren since all the things we were talking about happened quite a while before I met him.

Sid, Warren and Ellie in 2002

"I first *did* meet him in 2002 when he came and spoke to our church group in Yonkers. Warren had been a fireman in New York City and on duty on September 11, 2001, which was the day his world got turned upside down. A bunch of his fellow firemen were killed that day and Warren came pretty close to being killed himself while rescuing several people.

"He told me, when we met, that it brought him closer to God, which was one of the things that impressed me about him. Another thing was the fact that he was mostly raised by his Grandfather on a farm in rural Alabama and knew something about farming land.

"Saying that, I don't want to give the impression that my marriage to Warren was nothing but some kind of business arrangement. We were fond of each other and I was certain that our relationship would deepen over time.

"I inherited the piece of land you visited me on in 1995. Me and Sid visited my Aunt there with my folks when we were just little kids. My folks were fighting at the time then, and that wasn't so great, but the place she lived, an abandoned old town called Lumberton, was strange and interesting; and I did like my Aunt Kate. I could tell she liked me too. But even so, I was pretty surprised when she left the land to me!

"It originally had been a lot more than six acres too, but the state of New York had their eye on it for a housing development and contested the will. Finally in '02 a compromise agreement was reached, giving me six acres of it and me agreeing to sell the rest of it to the state of New York.

1987 Snooping on Aunt Kate's property.

"I'd already been thinking about the idea of making a farm of some sort on it, even before I met Warren, so when I heard he had farming experience and was such a nice, sweet guy, it was just starting to feel meant to be. Besides, I thought it would do Warren good to get away from all that New York 9/11 atmosphere.

"But, I guess, that was easier said than done. We'd no sooner got the house built, when Bush started the war in Iraq. Warren was all fired up to join the army and go over there. I was against it at first, but Warren said that if God had spared him the way he did on September 11, it must be a sign that it was meant for him to go over there. We'd both voted for George W. Bush because of his deep religious convictions and finally I began to see it his way. So we put the farm plan on hold for a year while Warren went and did his duty. Well, one year stretched on for three years until 2007, when Warren was killed.

"It was quite a blow. I guess my feelings for Warren ran a lot deeper than I realized!

"Another thing about it was, I'd worried about him but, at the same time, I'd had a really strong inner conviction that he'd be okay. And the fact is, his death kind of triggered a crisis of personal faith in me that I still really haven't come to terms with.

"Anyway, while grieving over it, I began looking over the property a little more than I had up to that time. I guess you could say it was a way for me to get away from feeling so bad about things.

"Looking around, it started to bring back a lot of memories of the time in 1987 when my folks brought me and Sid up here; and how we saw all the strange things that fascinated us so much as kids.

"Then recently, while looking around the old hotel Aunt Kate had lived in and cleaning out the room she'd slept in, I found something. It was a manuscript addressed to me! In a way it might have been kind of a sign that I didn't find it earlier, because then I probably wouldn't have been so receptive to some of the ideas it contains. Besides that, I've got to say, Kim, it's quite a story and, maybe, right up your alley."

Kate, Charles Varnay, and Rousseau on the French Riviera in 1919.

Well, Ellie is certainly right about that (to say the least!) and I am honored, and touched, that she has chosen me to present another story from the family archives of the amazing Whaleys.

Chapter One: Kate's story begins
Well, hello there, Ellie, I don't know how well you remember your Aunt Katherine. We didn't meet too many times. But I remember you
1987 The Whaleys visit Aunt Kate in Lumberton
HOTE
LOADING
TODAY
TODAY
BRAUNTON'S
and the time your parents brought you and Sidney for a visit some years back.
There wasn't much, I guess, for a couple of lively kids to do up here...

but I do remember how fascinated you were with that talking head I had and how disappointed you were when I told you it didn't talk any more.

Well, Ellie, life is full of disappointments. I've been waiting forty-eight years for that head to say something to me. Because if it did, I'd know that Mr. Varnay had finally returned to me as he said he would.

My parting with Mr. Varnay was not acrimonious. He was the finest gentleman I ever met. God knows he treated me better than any father ever did.

Charles Andreas Varnay was my teacher, my mentor and my very good friend. Do I show a trace of disappointment saying that? As if I somehow regret that he wasn't more than a friend? Well, I don't mean to. Mr. Varnay *was* more than a friend! More than a father but...

Oh, I hope you'll excuse an old woman, Ellie, if I ramble a bit, I'm not as sharp as I was once upon a time. To tell God's truth, I never was terribly bright and I'm afraid that's *why* I was such a disappointment to Mr. Varnay. I'm afraid he saw more in me than was really there! Although, thanks to him, I suppose I was more than I might have been.

A good deal of my life has been quite lonely. I never had children, though I doted on those of my brother, Andrew, and *his* grandsons, Garwood and, of course, your Father, Edward. And even though I didn't get to know you and Sidney very well, I was absolutely delighted, Ellie, when I heard about you two and your amazing rescue of Garwood and how it brought Edward and your Mother back together.*

You're a good girl, Ellie, and I'm proud of you. So you see, news *does* get up here. I have my television.

* See "The Sunshine Girl," in *Deitch's Pictorama*, 2008, Fantagraphics.

Of course, there isn't much doing in the way of news here in Lumberton these days. Oh, I forgot; I shouldn't call it Lumberton any more. All this land is officially a part of Big Flats* now. And there hasn't been a piece of lumber floating down the Chemung River in fifty years at least! The only thing I see on it now when I look out my window are kids on motorboats and the ferry passing by. All that forest land up river played out years ago.

You see, with no more trees coming down the river to be processed, Lumberton ceased to have any further reason to exist. All the mill hands moved on and their families with them. And all the saws and factory equipment were taken elsewhere too. The workers' shacks were mostly abandoned.

They all belonged to old Mr. Braunton. And when he died, he left the remains of his old boomtown to his two sons, Wolf and Karl. Then Wolf sold Karl liquor for the old Braunton Tavern, that he let Karl manage until Karl's liver gave out, which was some time around 1921.

That's when Mr. Varnay bought Lumberton; or what was left of it. He had all the old workers' shacks torn down, but kept most of the buildings on Lumberton's main street, including the old nickelodeon theater where I used to work.

I guess that old nickelodeon wasn't much, but it sure meant a lot to me when I was growing up. It was just an old converted livery stable where movies were

* A town west of Elmira in New York State.

shown. But it was also just about all the culture Lumberton ever really had.

Oh, there was once a library that Ann Kindling had set up, but that was really more of a clearing house where Lumberton's women mostly could borrow and swap copies of books by Bertha M. Clay, Laura Jean Libbey and Eden Southworth.*

When I was very young, I remember Mrs. Kindling used to have a Saturday story hour for the few children in town and I recall, with keen pleasure, hearing her read us adventures of D'Artagnan and so many others in weekly serial instalments.

Then about 1907, or maybe '08, the Gem Theater set up. The new movies were becoming more popular and, I guess, old Mr. Braunton saw getting a nickelodeon theater started as another way to get back some of the money he was paying his mill hands and also a way to give his sons, Wolf and Karl, something to do.

Wolf had been foreman of the sawmill until he had an accident, and Karl never did seem interested in much other than being drunk all the time.

I guess, in a way, that might have been Old Man Braunton's fault. He figured if he ran the bar he drank in, he might as well make the booze they drank and sell it too. So he set up his own still and put Karl in charge of it. Well, that idea of having Karl run the moonshine distillery sure backfired! Besides drinking up as much of the booze it produced as he could, he nearly burned the whole thing down! So Braunton set Karl up as manager of the Gem and since Wolf couldn't work in the mill any more, Braunton set him up projecting the Gem's films and also keeping an eye on Karl.

* Popular writers of women's "thriller" fiction of days gone by.

Now that we had movies, Lumberton's population took to them like bees to honey, and me too. Since there were getting to be a lot more kids in town, Mrs. Kindling switched from being the librarian to teaching school.

The school was just a one-room affair with no clear-cut grading system, but she did her best with Lumberton's coming generation. I could already read a little, but was excited by the idea of a real school.

Mrs. Kindling saw how eager I was to learn and, for the next few years, did her best to transfer all she knew into me, which was actually quite a bit; more than just McGuffey's Readers and the Bible, though we certainly did go through those with a fine-tooth comb. But there was also arithmetic, geography, elocution, and Shakespeare, too; the parts she deemed proper, anyway; and music; how to read and play it.

In time she got me to be a fair hand at the piano playing Brahms, Beethoven and my own personal favorite, Frederic Chopin.

I loved Ann Kindling. She was more than a mother ever could have been. You see, I never knew my real mother. And as for my father, well, he sure wasn't much. I know this is going to sound terrible, Ellie, but when my father was killed in an accident, at the mill, I was actually relieved even though I never let on. I was just about to turn fourteen when it happened and was starting to look like a woman; a thing not lost on Seamus Whaley, my drunken sot of a father.

If it hadn't been for Mrs. Kindling taking me in, when it happened, I prob-ably would have been packed off to the orphanage in Cascade City.

But she *did* take me in. And she said something to me at that time that I'll never forget. Basically she warned me to watch out for the ways of *man*kind, accent on the man part. Of course, I already saw what my own Father was like, and Mrs. Kindling said, in truth, the whole lot of them weren't much better, with only one thing on their mind, at least as far as women were concerned.

But it can also be a curse if you're not careful!

She told me that human beings as a group had a lot of potential and evidence of their progress was to be seen all around, but that good men were the exception to the rule.

Most of them are just a lot of two-footed animals without feathers!

Two-footed animals without feathers! That really stayed with me, being as it was just about the most cynical thing I ever heard Mrs. Kindling say.

I had been her prize student and was soon helping her at the school. And if she hadn't done such a good job teaching me music, I might have succeeded her as teacher when she died during that bad winter of 1915.

But when I had just turned eighteen the idea of teaching a bunch of brats, most of whom didn't even want to learn, didn't hold a lot of appeal for me. Even so, I did try to keep the school going that year.

Then, one day, coming out of the school after an especially trying day fending off the crude advances of some of the older boys, I saw something going on at the Gem that changed everything.

Chapter Two: The Isis
They were putting a whole new front on the theater.
And a brand new sign being put in place was even changing the Gem's name. It was going to be called the Isis now, which I later learned was the name of an Egyptian goddess.
In fact, on the sign was a small statue of a naked woman with an Egyptian headdress. It's out there yet, Ellie. You probably saw it.
LOADING DOCK# 2
BOX OFFICE A-75
TODAY
5¢
The man supervising all this was a slight, wiry-looking individual with red hair and freckles and he stopped to chat when he saw me.
He told me that his name was Abe Fortune and that Braunton had brought him in from Cascade City to give the movie house a new look.
When he said that, I told him I was thinking about going to Cascade City to try to get a job playing piano in one of the nickelodeon theaters there.
I asked him if he knew any-one over there to talk to and he said,
You're talking to him right now, Girly.

I was just about to send over to Cascade City for a piano player and here you are!

I didn't care for his cheap, familiar manner, but I was also beginning to feel that, unfortunately, this was just the way things were in this man's world and I might, at least, *try* to come to some accommodation with it *if* such a thing was possible.

So, when Abe Fortune asked me to have dinner with him, and to audition later for a job, I was suspicious, but accepted.

Well, the line of bull he dished out over dinner! (Pardon the expression, Ellie, but that's what it

seemed like to me.) To hear Abe Fortune tell it, he just about invented the movies all by himself. And he claimed to be bosom buddies with just about any star you could name. Clara Kimball Young and Mary Pickford* were old girlfriends of his, or so he implied.

* Two popular movie stars of the day.

By the time dinner was over and he was inviting me back over to the newly named Isis theater, I was ready to call the whole thing off, figuring it was all some plan to get fresh with me, but no!

Mr. Braunton met us out in front of the Isis and

inside, knock me over, was a new, upright piano! Up to this time Wolf and Karl just played old gramophone records, along with the movies, if they played anything at all, and the same old scratchy records at that. It was even kind of a relief, sometimes, when they didn't play anything.

Well, since Abe Fortune and Mr. Braunton seemed all business, I got right down to business too. I played some of my best Chopin things and tried some ragtime as well. They seemed pleased enough, but Abe said that he also wanted a sample of my singing, as the new Isis would also be presenting illustrated songs.

Now that *was* something. That may be something

you haven't heard about, Ellie, but back in those days, they would actually sing popular songs in a movie show, along with colored slides, that dramatized the lyrics. It was something like those videos on television that kids watch now, but illustrated songs were more refined, at least in my opinion.

Anyway, my singing voice wasn't bad. They had sheet music for a new song called "Peg O' My Heart." I sang it and got the job.

* * * * * *

I guess you could say 1913 was kind of a peak year in Lumberton. Mr. Braunton's lumber business was booming and Lumberton seemed more like a town than it ever had before. Not much of a town, but it did have a school and a general store (that Braunton owned, of course) along with a hotel, tavern, and Braunton's special pride, the Isis. By the following year, the workers at the mill more than doubled and Mr. Braunton was becoming wealthier than ever.

Figure it out for yourself. His workers paid him rent to live in his shacks, bought from his store, drank liquor in his tavern that came from his distillery. Anything they didn't spend that way or squander on women over in Cascade City, once a month, got spent at the Isis theater. And what with all the improvements, admission was up from a nickel to a dime now for everything but the Saturday matinee.

Braunton's two sons still worked there, but old Braunton made it crystal clear to them that Abe Fortune was running things. And to give Abe credit, he was doing a pretty good job.

Abe even talked Braunton into letting him do shows on Sunday. Up til' then, Braunton had kept the tavern and the movie show closed on Sundays, which wasn't really a Sabbath thing, because one thing Lumberton never did have was any kind of church. Mr. Braunton was just smart enough to realize that things ran better with his workers showing up on Monday, after their day off Sunday, without hangovers.

Working in a lumber mill had its hazards. I knew that first hand. I knew, for instance, that it was being liquored up on the job that killed my Father.

Anyway, like I said, we were going great guns at the Isis and it wasn't all just Abe Fortune. The fact is, the movies themselves were getting better all the time. For one thing, they were getting longer. Big ones were starting to come in on two and even three reels, and

* An especially huge hit for this popular actress in 1914.

And then there were the serials! They were adventure stories that ran once a week and usually took about fifteen episodes to tell their story. It was great for business because each episode would climax with the heroine in some kind of danger that seemed impossible to get out of, and you'd be wondering all week how she was going to do it.

The first really memorable one was "The Perils Of Pauline," with Pearl White. I guess I remember that one so well because I got to sing an illustrated song for it called "Poor Pauline," which came with just about the most beautiful colored slides I'd ever seen.

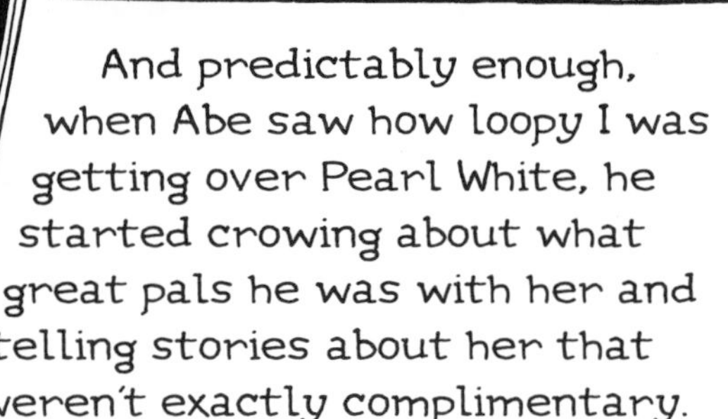

And predictably enough, when Abe saw how loopy I was getting over Pearl White, he started crowing about what great pals he was with her and telling stories about her that weren't exactly complimentary.

By this time I was actually going out with Abe a little; not that there was actually anything romantic going on between us. It was mostly just a convenient way to keep the two Braunton brothers from annoying me. Talk about your two-footed animals without feathers! They certainly filled that bill!

Not that Abe couldn't be a handful too, but he was a lot easier to handle than the two uncouth Brauntons. I didn't exactly like Abe, but then again, I didn't exactly dislike him either. For all of his hot air, he was still the most interesting man I'd met up to that time.

Even so, I sure wasn't buying all his bath water about knowing all those movie stars! It just seemed too obvious and an easy brag for him. Fat chance, I thought, that Pearl White, Ruth Roland, or any of the girls that starred in serials were ever going to come to Lumberton!

One big reason *why* I was so crazy about serials was that they usually had a woman as the star. And not some fluttery helpless young thing like in a lot of movies, but instead girls with real spirit who were just as good at getting out of tight scrapes as they were getting into them. I guess it was something that appealed to a lot of people because by 1915, it seemed like the whole country was serial crazy.

Besides Pearl White and Ruth Roland, there was Helen Holmes in "The Hazards of Helen." That one must have gone for a hundred episodes! Then there was Grace Cunard, who not only starred in the serials, but wrote the stories too.

But my supreme favorite, after I'd seen her in twenty episodes of "The Crimson Skull," was Molly O'Dare. Actually, I'd been a fan of hers, from even before. Her three-reeler, "The Fairy's Ball," from 1914, was just about the best movie I'd seen up to that time.

Of course, now that Molly O'Dare was a big serial queen, Abe was bragging of intimate friendship with her as well. So when I heard, in the summer of 1915, that Molly O'Dare actually was coming to Lumberton, you could have knocked me over! It seemed that she and her company were coming here to shoot what they called location stuff for a new serial she was making, called "The Danger Girl."

Well, not only was I out of my mind with excitement, I also figured this was where Mr. Abe Fortune would finally get his bluff called. But, to my surprise, Abe didn't seem at all put out and even said he'd been in on the deal with Braunton to bring the movie bunch in.

* See *Shadowland*, 2006, Fantagraphics Books

Chapter Three, the O'DARE AFFAIR!

Well, that really *is* a story worth telling. The movie crew came in on the night boat, the following week, at 3 a.m. and were already the talk of Lumberton by the time I got up. And while it wasn't exactly the way Abe told it, he really *did* know Molly O'Dare!

Not that it was the only surprise of the day. It was full of those and some disappointments too. The first and biggest surprise was that Abe actually had worked as a projectionist and occasional assistant cameraman at Molly O'Dare's New Jersey studio a few years earlier.

The first and biggest disappointment was that Molly O'Dare was nothing like I expected her to be. She and her crew were already settled in at Braunton's hotel when I met Abe out in front of the Isis that morning.

Abe seemed both eager and uneasy when he took me over to meet her.

Well, the first person we saw standing out front, ordering all sorts of strange people around, was a man Abe introduced as Doc Ledicker, who was in charge. He looked a little like a chubby version of Buffalo Bill.

He greeted me with great warmth and had that same sort of oozing familiarity that always put me off with Abe. I guess I was beginning to recognize a type.

When Abe asked about Molly, Doc Ledicker laughed, said we could find her upstairs and that we were welcome to her. And with that, he was off talking to some other people as Abe led me through the lobby and up to the second floor.

Molly O'Dare was clearly in the third room on the right, the same room I now live in. I say clearly because there was a team of people rushing in and out.

One person just ahead of us was a pinchy-looking woman carrying in a wig of long-flowing blonde locks that I instantly felt pretty sure must belong to Molly O'Dare.

Abe shoved me in right along behind her, which made us arrive before the great Molly O'Dare, just one second before her hair did! Oh, she had hair: brown, same as mine, all pinned up close to her head, which was covered in bright yellow make-up that I soon learned all movie actors wore so they'd photograph correctly.

As soon as she saw the girl with her hair, she yelled at her using words I won't repeat, though I clearly remember them as I do everything else that happened on that amazing day.

Next she tossed off the contents of a cup she held in one swallow and handed the empty cup to her slave of all work, who scurried out with it, which was the first time Molly's features formed into a smile, but with no real kindness in it and she made various comments to us, none of which were in any way complimentary or especially friendly.

Before Abe could get a word in, the sullen maid returned and handed Molly her mug full of something that smelled strongly of alcohol. Just then, Doc Ledicker came in.

When he saw the reeking mug in Molly's hand, he did not look happy, but did his best to assume a civil manner while chiding her about her "toddies." Whatever they consisted of, apparently the agreement was, they weren't to be taken before noon. As it was 8:30 a.m., these "toddies" definitely were in forbidden territory.

Her retort, again, was in words I will not repeat; nor did Doc Ledicker stay to hear them. But, as he left the room, to my utter horror, Abe followed him out.

I wasn't exactly alone with her. Her maid was fitting a wig on and Molly, between swallows, was allowing another person to begin painting and rouging her face.

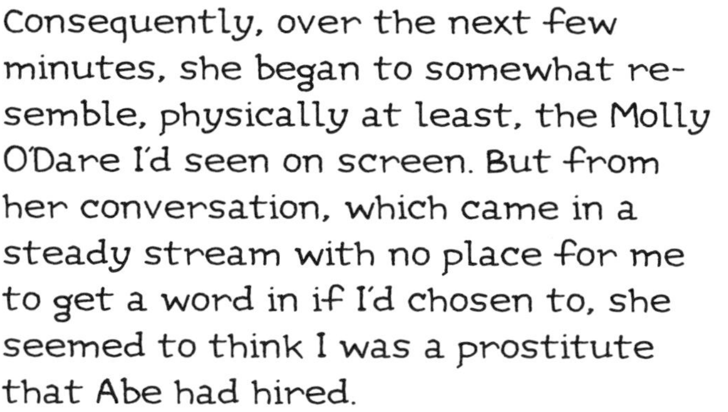

Consequently, over the next few minutes, she began to somewhat resemble, physically at least, the Molly O'Dare I'd seen on screen. But from her conversation, which came in a steady stream with no place for me to get a word in if I'd chosen to, she seemed to think I was a prostitute that Abe had hired.

When I finally did manage to stammer out that it was not true, she broke out into a loud, raucous laugh. I can still hear the echo of that booming laugh all these years later, the joke apparently being that Abe Feinstein, as she called him, couldn't possibly be consorting with a girl who wasn't being paid for it.

I wasn't really sure if this was just her way of giving me the needle or where the conversation would have gone from there, when Abe signaled to me to come out in the hall where he and Doc Ledicker had been talking.

I ran out of that room like I'd been shot out. I was never so glad to see Abe in my life. It turned out that Abe had convinced Doc Ledicker to get me to substitute for Molly in the scenes at the mill since Molly was somewhat "under the weather," as Doc Ledicker politely put it.

While Doc went in to deal with Molly, Abe started really laying it on. How this was a big chance and that he'd even talked Doc into taking a few extra shots of me as a screen test and so on.

I don't remember it all because the growing noise of conversation between Doc and Molly got louder and louder until suddenly Doc just tore the blonde wig right off her head and said,

Before I knew it, the makeup man was slap-ping that yellow makeup on my face and they were fitting Molly's wig onto me. I wasn't feeling good about any of this and it didn't help one bit that Molly was furious. As Doc led her away, she had a lot to say which I won't repeat.

Allen Rollins, Molly's leading man, seemed to think

it was all a big joke the way I'd "upstaged" Molly, as he put it.

But I felt sorry for her in spite of everything and I wasn't really liking what I'd seen so far of these movie people.

Well, the rest of the day could have been like a dream but it was actually closer to a nightmare!

By the time I was made up and dressed, they were all set to start shooting in the number one mill. The idea of the scene was that Molly was tied to a big log being fed into one of the mill's large saw blades.

As I was being tied down, I wasn't feeling any too good about things, but Abe told me not to worry, The big blade was only going half speed. Abe explained that they'd crank it slower to make it look faster on screen. But I was scared, half speed or not, as Allen Rollins, also moving slower, headed for the big power switch on the log feed.

Well, as it turned out, I had good reason to be scared. Just as he was about to switch off the log feed,

Allen Rollins slipped on a grease stain!

I probably would have been killed if it hadn't been for the action of the company's makeup man

who was covering the shot on a second camera! Quick as a flash, he ran to the switch and stopped the log feed just in time!

It was as narrow an escape as any cliffhanger I ever saw in a serial! I was all in one piece, but the blade had just begun to shred Molly's wig!

That should have been enough excitement for one day, but there was more! Abe and Doc Ledicker were all over me with solicitous concern after the fact, for all the good they'd done me.

In fact, within seconds, Doc was bawling out my rescuer for knocking over his camera as he rescued me, while Abe steered me back over to the Isis.

Word had definitely spread about Molly O'Dare being in town, because as we made our way to the Isis, a crowd was already forming of people who'd heard that Molly O'Dare would appear there. I even saw my brother Andrew in the crowd there with a bunch of his rowdy pals from up river.

Now, Ellie, if you're wondering why I haven't said much about Andy, 'til now, it's because I never saw much of him. He was six years older than me and had a job in the lumber camps up river which kept him out of Lumberton most of the time except for every few months when logs were floated down the Chemung river. It got him away from our no-good father, but since then, for all I could see, he'd turned into just another dumb, low-life logger himself!

Once Abe and I got inside, I could see Abe and Doc Ledicker had been busy as beavers getting this Molly O'Dare personal appearance together. They'd rigged a large paper screen about two feet in front of the regular one. The idea was that I would stand next to the paper screen as it showed different colored slides with scenes from Molly's movies projected on it, while I sang the verse of a new song that Abe had cooked up, called "Marvelous Molly."

I was to lead the audience in singing the song's chorus. Then, at the very end,

Molly herself would burst through the screen and sing the song's last line, which was, "I'm marvelous Molly O'Dare."

These slides flashed on screen as Kate sang the verse to Marvelous Molly*

Abe and I went over the song for the rest of the afternoon and had it down pretty good. But then about half an hour before the show, Doc Ledicker came running in looking pale and worried.

Molly O'Dare was nowhere to be found, which

* Words and music © 1915 by Abe Fortune

wasn't good news, because we had a big crowd outside. After Doc ran out again, Abe did his best to calm me down.
Listen, this could be your big break!
He told me that Doc Ledicker had been impressed with my work at the sawmill and,
You saw how played out that old has-been O'Dare is.
Think about it. This could be *your* hour!
I didn't like it. I didn't think Molly O'Dare was a very nice person, but I wasn't keen on getting into the environment that made her that way either.
Marvelous Molly O'Dare, she always plays right on the square. She never backs down when the time comes to fight. She faces all trouble that comes into sight. In a tight spot, when things get hot, she laughs at all trouble and care. For she is the one girl, that wonderful fun girl, she's marvelous Molly O'Dare!
But, for the time being I put myself in Abe's hands. He said the thing to do just then was to rework things so I
sang the last line of the song myself. And then we'd just go right into the next episode of "Who Pays?" with Ruth Roland, which was the serial we were showing that week and hope to heaven that those rowdy lumberjacks wouldn't tear the Isis down when Molly was a no-show.
Needless to say, that night I was a little nervous when I started singing, but the crowd seemed to like it, and joined in heartily when I led them in the chorus. In fact, I was beginning to think things would turn out just fine. Then, as we were about to hit the last line of the song, to my total shock, Molly O'Dare did burst through the paper screen, knocking me right on my face as she delivered the last line of the song!

I'm marvelous MOLLY O'DARE!
What's more, she looked absolutely great; just like she did in the movies!
Marvelous Molly O'Dare.
She always plays
right on the square.
She
when
She
that
In a tight spot,
when things get
she laughs at all
trouble and care.
For she is the one
girl,
marvelous
The cheering at the Isis was unbelievable and didn't stop for a long time. It was ten minutes before we could start the movie.
By the time I got up and Molly put her arm around me and kissed me on the cheek, I could smell alcohol on her breath as she whispered,
(Try and upstage me again, you little bitch, and you'll get worse than that.)

I was in a total daze when I played for episode 12 of "Who Pays?", which went over especially well as it was all about the lumber business. While it played, I heard a retching noise like someone throwing up and was pretty sure it had to be Molly O'Dare.

Sure enough, a few minutes later, I saw Abe and Doc Ledicker hustle her out and she was back to not looking so good.

After the show, Abe came back over to me, looking ecstatic.

Kid, you are in!

He told me he had it all fixed with Ledicker for both of us to leave

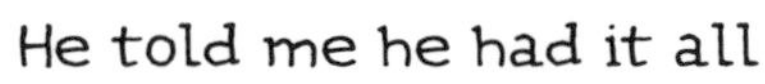

that night with the movie troupe. He told me Doc Ledicker had been very impressed with me and was eager to build me up as a serial star. He told me the idea was to build me up as a kind of insurance to keep Molly O'Dare in line.

Well, I told Abe I didn't like the sound of that one single bit. As far as I was concerned, my one day in the movie world would hold me for quite a while, thank you very much!

I could see that Abe was disappointed and, for a moment, I wavered, asking him if my refusal was going to ruin his chance.

But Abe laughed at me and said,

Don't flatter yourself. I'll just tell Molly it was me that talked you out of coming.

He winked at me and, taking full advantage of my flustered state, kissed me on the cheek, a thing he'd never dared to do before, then hurried out before I could do or say anything.

I heard the next day that they all left on the 3 a.m. night-boat and I never saw Abe, Doc Ledicker, or Molly O'Dare again.

I was sorry when I heard about her and Doc Ledicker being lost at sea in 1922* but not exactly surprised.

The events of that day sure changed my idea about the movies. Not that I stopped liking them, but I did remember something Mrs. Kindling once said to me about not taking them quite so seriously, and I was beginning to see what she meant by that.

And, after meeting Molly O'Dare, I also thought about that other thing Mrs. Kindling told me and began to think that perhaps men weren't necessarily the only two-footed animals without feathers!

After saying that, it may strike you as a contradiction that I was still a big fan of the movies, including ones starring Molly O'Dare, but it's true!

* See *Shadowland*, 2006, Fantagraphics.

And I missed Abe Fortune, too. Whatever his faults may have been, he was never boring, and now with him gone, the burden of running the Isis was on my shoulders.

Mr. Braunton told me I could run it my way and if his sons got out of line, I had only to say the word and he'd fire both of them and bring in new help from Cascade City.

It all went good as his word except now old Braunton himself was paying more attention to me and would always be up in his box leering at me when I sang the illustrated songs.

One interesting thing did occur, though, about four months later. We got Molly O'Dare's serial, "The Danger Girl," and did we do some business! One thing I noticed right away was that Abe Fortune got credit on screen for writing the story. In fact, I even spotted him playing a small role in the first episode, so I guess he was all set.

But the really surprising thing, for me, was how much I still enjoyed watching Molly O'Dare! She was *great* in "The Danger Girl" – better than ever! I got sucked right in and, of course, I couldn't wait to see the saw mill episode, and that was a total surprise. The way it worked now, according to Abe Fortune's new script, was that Allen Rollins was tied on a log feeder to a whirling buzz saw and Molly came in and rescued *him*.

Well, the buzz saw set wasn't quite accurate, but I have to say, the scene was great, and much more what you'd expect from the Molly O'Dare character.

But, like I said, my actual situation was going downhill and I was again thinking it was time to leave Lumberton.

I hadn't yet figured out how I was going to do it, though, when Charles Andreas Varnay came to town and showed me the way.

The first time I saw Charles Andreas Varnay was on a cold April morning in 1916. It was 6 a.m. and I was on my way to the school house. Yes, I was still teaching school, too, waiting for the replacement that Mr. Braunton never seemed to get around to hiring. Frankly, I think it was just a sneaky way of his to try to keep me in Lumberton! As I passed by, I noticed several large crates out in front of the hotel and a number of people loitering about. The ones I talked to seemed to think it might be another movie crew, and after I got a good look at Mr. Varnay, I thought it might be true, but all it was was one man and one very alert-looking dog.

The dog seemed to be a breed I wasn't familiar with, which should have meant mutt. Well, maybe so, but the dog carried himself like no dog I'd ever seen! He had the carriage of a thoroughbred horse and the most alert, intelligent face I could ever remember seeing on a dog. That alone would have got my attention but the real surprise was the dog's master!

He was a trim-looking gentleman, somewhat less than average height. But that scarcely begins to describe him! He might have been fifty years old, though I never did find out how old Mr. Varnay really was.

The really strange thing about him was that he dressed like something out of a costume drama of the 18th century, with one of those powdered wigs and a fur-trimmed three-cornered hat on top of it. Add to that large owlish glasses, high boots, and a long coat and you begin to have a picture of Mr. Varnay.

It was shocking how quiet everything got as he walked, in a very stately way, into the hotel and registered! As he signed the hotel book, the dog turned and looked at us as if warning us not to crowd his master. Then he turned to the dog and said, "Ici Rousseau!"

He gave Billy Warren a silver dollar to carry his trunk, and he and the dog proceeded upstairs.

That's when we all rushed to the hotel desk. The name signed to the register, in a beautiful hand, was Charles Andreas Varnay and in parentheses (Lecturer on Natural Enlightenment). And he paid in advance for a week!

Well, to say this caused a sensation is to put it mildly. I later heard that he had his meals sent up to his room from Bartlett's Eats. And when, not surprisingly, that proved unsatisfactory, he hired Ellen Maydew to cook for him from special recipes he supplied her with.

And that was the last anyone saw of Mr. Varnay for several days! His meals were left outside his room door. Later Ellen or her son, Martin, would pick up the dishes outside the door and there would be two silver dollars on the tray with them.

Ellen did say she thought she heard Mr. Varnay having a conversation with someone in French, one time when picking up the dishes.

And that seemed strange since Mr. Welford, who ran the hotel for Braunton, saw no one coming or going from Mr. Varnay's room.

He did leave a message, along with his empty dishes, for Ellen to find someone and pay them one dollar a day to walk his dog for an hour at 5 p.m. We all watched each day, at five, as the stately dog led Ellen's son into an alley where the dog did his "business" with more dignity and dispatch than one usually associates with the act of defecation.

The tension broke on the third day of Mr. Varnay's visit in a surprising way. It was Wednesday and, at the Isis, we were showing the latest episode of Pearl White's great serial, "The Iron Claw." Everyone, myself included, thought it was just about the greatest serial ever. Pearl was being generally tormented by the Iron Claw, who was missing one hand and had a curved metal spike in place of it. He had a strange, hand-shaped scar on his face that had something to do with an ancient grudge against Pearl's family. But a mysterious masked stranger, known only as the Laughing Mask, was on hand each week to protect Pearl. You can be certain that everyone that year, not just in Lumberton, but the entire nation, wanted to know who the Laughing Mask was.

Well, to the surprise of everyone, Mr. Varnay and his dog, Rousseau, were there that night to see the show! He'd rented the private box that Mr. Braunton usually used. That must have taken some doing, but there they were.

And that was strange too. Usually when Mr. Braunton leered at me when I sang, it always made me uncomfortable. But when I glanced up and saw Mr. Varnay and Rousseau studying me, it had quite the opposite effect. Instead, I felt a genuine warmth coming from them that actually seemed to make me sing better.

When the new episode of "The Iron Claw" came on, a good one, I glanced up at them several times while playing for it and noticed that Mr. Varnay seemed to be watching and taking notes. However, when the episode was over, he and Rousseau didn't stay for the rest of the show.
The Laughing Mask, Pearl White's mysterious protector in "The Iron Claw."
Lecture
Sunday 8:00 P.M.
Human Progress
From Apehood
Enlightenment
Free
Admission
When the show let out, I noticed a crowd gathering over by the empty house next to the hotel that had once been a dry goods store. Tacked to the front door was a notice advertising a lecture to be given the following Sunday evening in the store by Mr. Varnay. The name of the lecture was "Human Progress: From Apehood to Enlightenment; Admission free." What a sensation that caused!
TODAY!
William S. Hart
Hell's Hinges
The Laughing Mask?

I for one was mighty glad there was no show on Sunday, because that was one lecture I just had to see! It was the talk of the town and the last we saw of Mr. Varnay until Sunday.
The daily meals were brought. The dog-walking went on, as did more reports of strange occasional conversations in French being heard in Mr. Varnay's room. But mostly all was quiet in there.
Then came Sunday, and you should have seen it! Clearly the word of the mysterious Mr. Varnay had spread, because men from the camps up river even showed up and mostly couldn't get in. I did manage to get my brother Andrew and a few of his pals in, though. You see, three nights after Varnay's sign was posted, I received a special invitation. At first glance I thought it was engraved. But then I remembered the fine hand Varnay signed the hotel register with.
H
Sure enough, when I looked closer I realized he'd written it himself.
Admit Katherine Whaley and 4 of her friends C.A.V.

Mr. Varnay was standing at the door, letting one person at a time enter and making a notation in a small notebook each time.

When I showed up with my brother and his friends, he bowed,

turned to Rousseau, made a sign to him and told us to follow the dog in to our reserved seats up in front.

Every other seat in the place was taken, with even a dozen or so people standing in back. It all got off to a good start.

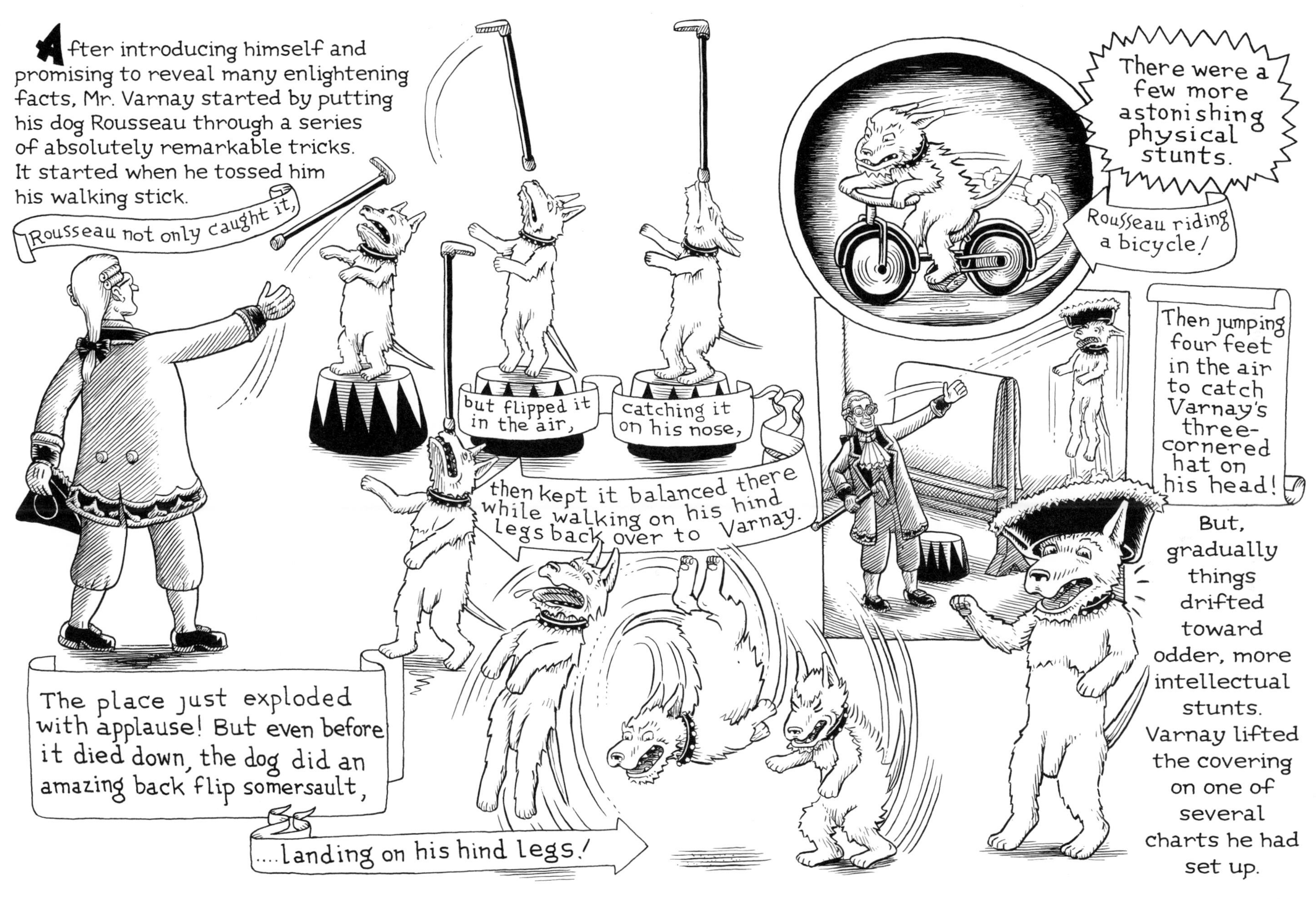
After introducing himself and promising to reveal many enlightening facts, Mr. Varnay started by putting his dog Rousseau through a series of absolutely remarkable tricks. It started when he tossed him his walking stick.
Rousseau not only caught it,
but flipped it in the air,
catching it on his nose,
then kept it balanced there while walking on his hind legs back over to Varnay.
The place just exploded with applause! But even before it died down, the dog did an amazing back flip somersault,
....landing on his hind legs!
There were a few more astonishing physical stunts.
Rousseau riding a bicycle!
Then jumping four feet in the air to catch Varnay's three-cornered hat on his head!
But, gradually things drifted toward odder, more intellectual stunts. Varnay lifted the covering on one of several charts he had set up.

The first one had the names of four philosophers with numbers in front of their names. Varnay asked the dog which of them he was named for. The dog immediately barked four times, which coincided with Rousseau, the fourth name on the list.

This was received with polite applause, but as the questions proceeded, the audience was beginning to show signs of restlessness. One question got my attention, though. At one point he asked Rousseau what philosopher referred to certain debased types of humanity as two-legged animals without feathers. Well, I would have said Ann Kindling, so that shows how much I knew. Rousseau, on the other hand, barked out the Greek philosopher, Plato, out of six choices he was given.

At about this point the lecture took an even more pedantic turn. Varnay bowed to Rousseau and thanked him. Rousseau nodded back.

Then began the real meat of Varnay's presentation, which essentially ran like this. He told us that Rousseau was the painstaking result of years of careful breeding with the object of accelerating evolving canine development.

As he spoke, he unfurled various pictorial charts to illustrate this point, starting with one showing dog development, stating that dogs, like all earthly creatures in our universe, were in a state of evolving development.

By this time there were more signs of restlessness in the crowd, though they seemed to become slightly more interested when he got to charts showing the evolution of men and women, first from one-celled creatures to apes, then from ape to human. This probably had more to do with the drawings of naked men and women than with what he was actually saying.

However, this regained attention soon grew to jeering hostility as he continued. He told us that while humans were the most developed of earth's creatures, we were still much flawed. He said that humans, like his dog, could be similarly improved and elevated to the high destiny awaiting them with the same kind of careful breeding that developed his dog, Rousseau.

That didn't go over any too well; and it got worse! Unfurling yet another chart, Varnay told us that right now, in the human species, women were clearly more highly evolved than men and, yes,

the charts definitely stressed the less apelike appearance of women.

You could hear the hostility rumbling through the room as he pointed out the fallacy of having less evolved men running things in this world.

threw a rotten tomato at Varnay! He deftly dodged

it and it hit the chart. And that's when complete

mayhem broke out!
What was particularly troubling to me was that my brother, Andrew, seemed to be one of the troublemakers.
THE MARCH OF HUMANITY
When someone headed for what looked like a statue draped with a piece of cloth, Rousseau got out in front of it and held the man at bay with a savage warning snarl.

Then, when another man produced a gun and was about to fire it at Rousseau, Varnay went into action. In a flash, he pulled a sword from out of his walking stick and stabbed the man's gun hand. The man howled in pain as he dropped the weapon.

I yelled at the advancing crowd, to no avail. When I again saw Andrew among them, I ran to him and said,

I can only thank providence that my appeal got through to him. Somehow between us and Rousseau, we managed to clear the room. And I finally managed to get Andrew to leave too.

I must say, Mr. Varnay looked pretty disheveled. Both his glasses and wig had been knocked off but, surprisingly, without them, there was something eerily familiar looking about him! I suddenly had the nagging feeling that I'd seen him somewhere before!

He went to the door, signaled Rousseau to follow him, opened it, and the dog walked out. I later learned that Rousseau stood sentry against further intrusions from the disgruntled crowd outside.

Then Mr. Varnay turned back toward me and that's when it hit me! His head was shaved and he had no mustache, but I felt pretty sure that Mr. Varnay and the make-up man from Molly O'Dare's film crew, who saved my life at the sawmill, were one and the same person!

When I confronted him about this, he readily admitted it was true, but hastened to add that the man in the film crew was the disguise,

Oh my lord, Ellie, I won't lie to you. By this time my poor brain was positively swirling. And as I looked at this strange man in his utterly improbable 18th-century get-up, I began to seriously consider that I might be in the hands of a maniac!

He must have seen this in my expression and in an effectively soothing manner, he began to explain himself.

Katherine, I realize all that has happened must strike you as highly unusual. How could it be otherwise?

He was certainly right about that, and at this point I still wasn't sure that he wasn't deranged. But I was also starting to calm down. In fact, I was even quite eager and fascinated to hear the rest of what he had to say.

He told me that he'd been pretty certain all along that everything that just happened would occur exactly as it had.

Then, covering the door window with his handkerchief, he said,

I'm afraid most of your neighbors out there are not quite ready for the message I bring.

He told me that I, on the other hand, by my actions that day, had shown my eminent fitness to aid him in the project he had in mind. Quite frankly I was still unsure of this man's mental condition, but there was a kind of nobility about him that seemed to be saying to me that if this man was mad, it was a divine madness. Clearly, I was affected by him in a way that no other person had affected me before!

And I guess, Ellie, that's why what happened next happened the way it did. The next thing that did happen, and I hope this won't shock you, Ellie, was that Mr. Varnay then, very politely and respectfully, I might add, asked me to remove all of my clothes!

Just as surprising, to me, was the fact that I actually proceeded to do so without hesitation. I won't deny that I found this to be a shocking request, but I also will not deny that at this point, crazy or not, I was beginning to be very attracted to this man! The manner in which he made the request certainly didn't match any attempts at seduction that I'd ever read about in books, but in all honesty my feeling at that moment was that if this *was* seduction, then so be it.

Well, it wasn't seduction and I'd be less than truthful if I didn't confess to feeling sort of disappointed about it.

As I stood there naked before him, he viewed me for several moments in what seemed like a kind of awed reverence, but suddenly he

seemed to snap out of it. Then, with a tape measure and in a very methodical way, he began to take all of my physical measurements!

He started at my feet and slowly worked his way up, taking particular care with the various widths of my head and skull. At this point, I really was starting to be put off by all this strangeness and was kind of mad at myself for being so stupid as to go along with it! Varnay, on the other hand, seemed quite gratified as he recorded each of my measurements into a little notebook.

When he was done, he politely asked me to dress again, which I was willing enough to do. I was getting cold standing there naked like that for so long! Needless to say, I was cooling down in other respects as well.

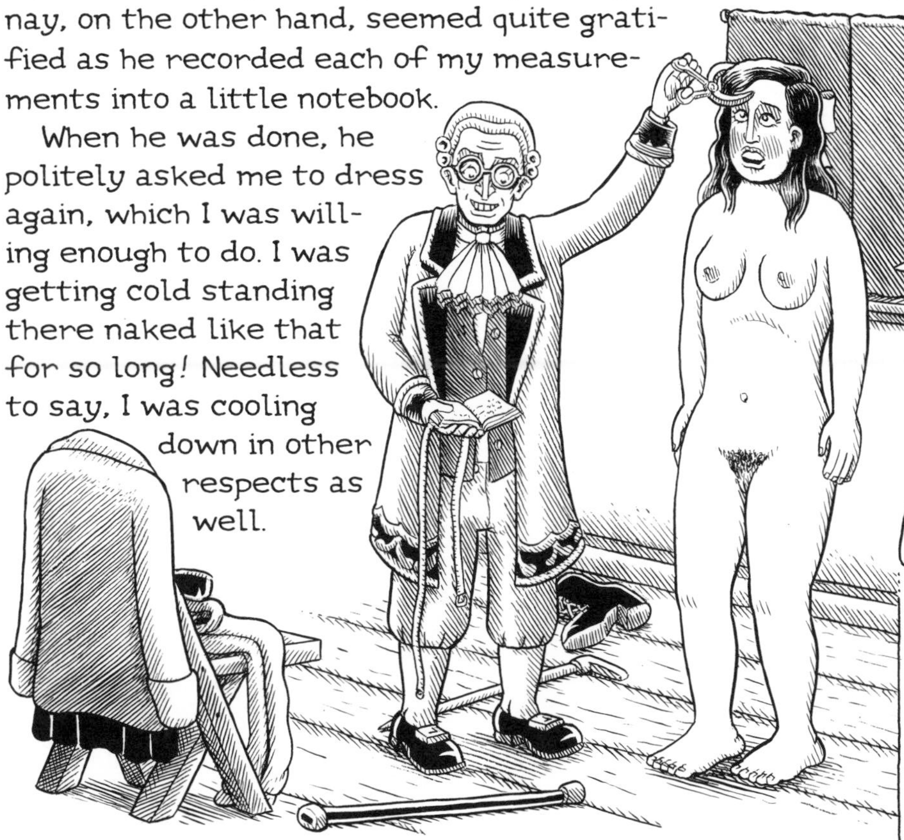

Once I was again dressed, he went over to the large draped object that looked like some kind of statue and pulled the cloth away, which just might have been the biggest shock of all!

There before me was a nude statue that, in every respect, looked just like me!

It was the very same statue, Ellie, that I once discovered you and Sidney looking at. I'm sure you remember it. She was holding what looked like some kind of urn. And at her feet there were six others. On the base of the statue was the motto, "Let There Be Enlightenment."

Mr. Varnay explained to me that the statue was a copy of one he'd found many years before in France. He told me that allegorically she represented the Goddess of Enlightenment. What he meant by that was that she wasn't exactly meant to be worshipped, but rather to symbolize a sort of human ideal.

The way Mr. Varnay explained it was,

And with that he launched into the rest of his lecture for me, his audience of one! He unfurled another chart itemizing recent human development as he saw it. He explained to me that 19th-century breakthroughs such as harnessing electricity, photography, and the ability to record sound, to name just a few examples, all had great potential toward furthering human progress.

But he went on to say that the greatest stumbling block getting in the way of this was other, more negative progress, specifically the development of great weapons of destruction, all of which were controlled by insufficiently evolved men.

This, he said, was the great problem that had to be overcome if the human race was ever going to continue to evolve in a good and positive direction. For this to happen, he said, it was necessary for a new age of revelation to be launched.

Oh my! The more he spoke, the more something deep inside of me seemed to be thrillingly responding to this man in spite of the fact that, really, I had only the sketchiest idea of what he was talking about.

But, as if reading my mind, he hastened to assure me that I needn't worry if complete understanding eluded me just then.

All these things will soon be made clear to you.

I guess that must have been the official end of his talk, because now Mr. Varnay began to pack all the various charts and props. And I must say, if the sole objective of his talk was to enlist me in his cause, a cause I still didn't really understand, I'd have to call it a roaring success. Because from that moment on, I was bound and determined to link my destiny with his and to follow that destiny wherever it might lead me.

As he continued to pack, he told me that until today, even though he was pretty certain that I was the right person to help him, he still had to be absolutely sure. That was the reason, he said, that he made the lecture so deliberately provocative.

I needed to see how you would respond in a situation of that kind.

And he now assured me that my forthright actions during the earlier part of the lecture more than satisfied him on that account.

Just then, what sounded like an automobile horn was heard outside, followed by two lively barks from Rousseau,

Come, it is time for us to depart, he said, walking to the door. When he opened it, I saw a colored man in a chauffeur's uniform, who gave Mr. Varnay a smart salute. Then he and Mr. Varnay grabbed opposite ends of his now packed box and carried it out.

As I followed, they loaded it into a large wagon that was hitched to a large touring car.

When I realized they were going to leave the nude statue behind, I admit I felt a twinge of panic. I didn't pose for it and it wasn't really me, but even so! But before I could ask about it, Mr. Varnay told me it was just a plaster copy of the original and had served its purpose.

Still, I couldn't help being a bit disturbed by this and wondered at the sensation it would make when the citizens of Lumberton saw it!

There was quite a crowd outside, but no one attempted to interfere with our departure. However, before I got into the car, I saw my brother and felt I couldn't leave without one last word with him.

While we had never really known each other very well, his actions that day seemed to me to have begun at least to form kind of a bond between us. And my one regret about leaving this way was that I wouldn't have an opportunity to improve that bond. I kissed him good-bye and told him not to worry – that strange as all this might seem, I firmly believed that all would be well.

And suddenly we were off to where I knew not. Even though I was pretty sure I believed what I just told Andrew, as I sat in the back seat of the car and snuggled my head on Mr. Varnay's shoulder, I didn't really get the reassurance I was looking for!

As the car slowly wheeled down Lumberton's main street, I could sense an uneasiness in him even as he kissed me lightly on the cheek.

He turned and looked at me with a rather wistfully sad expression and said that it was important for me to realize that there could never be any sort of physical relationship between us.

Of that, my dear, I assure you I am quite... unworthy.

He told me that instead I should try to regard him as more of a father and that, like a good father, he would seek out and find the perfect man for me. I didn't really know what to say to this.

Sensing my confusion, he put his arm around me and told me that I mustn't worry. Well, just then that seemed to be a pretty tall order!

Even so, I actually did feel somewhat comforted. After all, I supposed I could, at least, feel pretty sure, under these highly unusual circumstances, that he really did like me – as a person, I mean.

Chapter Five : The Secret of the Seven Urns.

Finally, I drifted off to sleep with his arm still around me. And it was still around me when we finally arrived at our destination. We must have been riding all night, because

it was a new morning as we got out of the car in front of a rather impressive-looking house.

Which I later learned was in the small Westchester County village of Irvington, New York.

As we went in, Mr. Varnay explained he was just renting the place for a few weeks while he conducted some business in New York City. He did not, however, explain where our final destination would be.

Mr. Varnay had actually provided me with a maid, a pleasant negro girl named Marie, who I later learned was married to Lionel, the chauffeur. Marie told me that they had been engaged a few weeks earlier, along with Weltman, the butler, from an employment agency in New York City.

Marie led me to a beautifully furnished room, and for the first time I became aware of the grimy condition I was in from my long ride. And suddenly the alarming reality that I'd left all my belongings back in Lumberton crashed upon me!

Good God! What kind of spell had this man cast over me?

Marie, seeing my anxiety, smiled, opened a closet door and beckoned me to come look.

To say that I was surprised hardly does credit to what the sight of all of those dresses, hats, shoes and underthings did to me!

And everything was a perfect fit! And I must say, to suddenly be living in this kind of luxury was very heady stuff!
You must understand, Ellie, that up to then even a thing like indoor plumbing, that everyone takes for granted now, was all quite new to me. And now here I was in a fine house being waited on by servants!

We were served in the dining room that really did seem ominously large for just the two of us. Well, there was Rousseau perched to the left of Mr. Varnay, waiting patiently for a nod from him to begin eating, which got a disapproving stare from Weltman.

Afterwards, Mr. Varnay asked me to join him in the study. When Rousseau began to follow, Mr. Varnay signaled for him to stay, which only made me more nervous. As I followed Mr. Varnay down a long hall,

...the unpleasant thought started bobbing up in my mind that perhaps the other shoe was about to fall.

The way he made me strip naked in Lumberton, the gloomy mansion we now found ourselves in, the locked door and the strange 18th-century costume he wore. By that time I was weeping uncontrollably. Varnay went to the door and unlocked it. When I looked back at him, he seemed so deflated and crestfallen that I began to feel a twinge of regret over my outburst. And when he approached me and put his arms around me, I let him, even as I continued to weep.

After a few moments he gently apologized, saying he understood my misgivings, and standing away from me, he said,

He told me that his unusual wardrobe was an homage of sorts to the 18th century Age of Enlightenment, which was a period of history he felt a strong affinity for.

After giving me a moment to collect myself, he began to tell me the fascinating story of his early life. He told me that, as a boy in France, he had been a sickly child. And at the age of fourteen, he had contracted a virulent fever that nearly killed him.
In the delirium brought on by this fever, he said an angel appeared. She told him that this fever would soon break and that he would awaken to find himself, henceforth, in perfect, robust health.
The angel went on to say that periodically, over the next few years, he would experience a series of dreams instructing him to perform various tasks.
He was to follow these instructions to the letter, for by so doing, he would build a conduit that would guide him to a higher knowledge of things.
The first predictions proved to be marvelously true, for when he awoke the next morning, his health was more than restored.
I felt a measure of vigorous health such as I never before experienced and that I continue to enjoy to this very day!

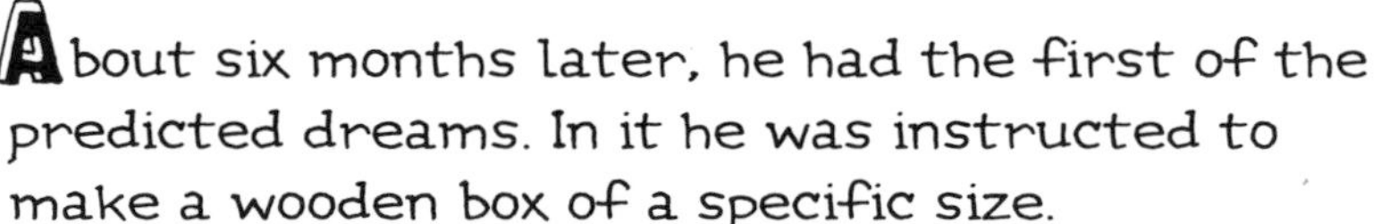

About six months later, he had the first of the predicted dreams. In it he was instructed to make a wooden box of a specific size.

For two long years he kept the box and waited. Just as he was about to despair of ever knowing more, a second dream came.

This time he was told to carve a block of wood, leaving an open space where the lower jaw should be, and not to worry about the head's appearance – that the details would naturally come to him as he carved.

In subsequent dreams that came with more frequency, he was told how to paint the head and finally to carve a lower jaw to fit into the head, much like those seen in ventriloquist dolls, except that this head had no mechanism in it to move the mouth.

At this point Mr. Varnay removed a sliding panel from the front of the first box and revealed the talking head, the very one, Ellie, that you were so curious about during your visit with me.

And this is the result of my labors

In a final dream, he was told the boxed head would become for him a channeling vehicle, meaning that it would speak to him and instruct him.

This began to happen almost immediately. From the start, Varnay told me, the words spoken by the head clearly were actually coming from himself, which was what the dream meant by the term "channeling vehicle." The head merely seemed to be strangely personifying a prophetic inner voice coming from somewhere within Varnay himself.

Did that mean this was all then just an elaborate form of madness? Well, judge for yourself. For one thing, Varnay told me (and I later witnessed this myself) the jaw moved, with no outside help, in perfect sync with the strange voice coming from Mr. Varnay! But most remarkable were the results of the instructions he began to receive.

Specifically, he was instructed to go to a certain wooded spot in the French countryside and to begin digging there.

The talking head informed him that these things had belonged to the famous French Revolution figure Robespierre,* who had been a member of a mysterious deist cult. Mr. Varnay explained to me that during the 18th century there were various such cults who were admirers of the ethical teachings of Jesus Christ. But these deists felt that Christ's story as it is told in the Bible had been tampered with to the point that Christ's message was buried under a lot of mumbo jumbo that made the story irrational and little more than a fairy tale. The particular cult that Robespierre belonged to were guardians of seven urns handed down from antiquity that were supposed to contain information that would one day reveal Christ's teachings in their purest, unaltered state exactly as they came from the master's own lips.

These teachings would be revealed at a critical moment when humanity most urgently needed to hear them.

But the great mystery of the urns was that they were completely empty, making many feel that whatever information they may have contained was now lost. However, the tradition handed down with these urns was that the message they contained was not lost and that they who secretly guarded and preserved these urns should not be troubled by this apparent contradiction.

What's more, in the true tradition of deism, it was felt that when this information was revealed, it would not come about in some supernatural way, but that it would happen in an entirely natural and scientific manner.

When Robespierre was swept up into the French Revolution's Reign of Terror, where he met his fate like so many others in that sadly

Robespierre

Maximilien Robespierre*
1758 - 1794
Idealist French leader. His excessive zeal was a key factor in the French Revolution's Reign of Terror, which ironically claimed him as one of its many victims. -K.D.

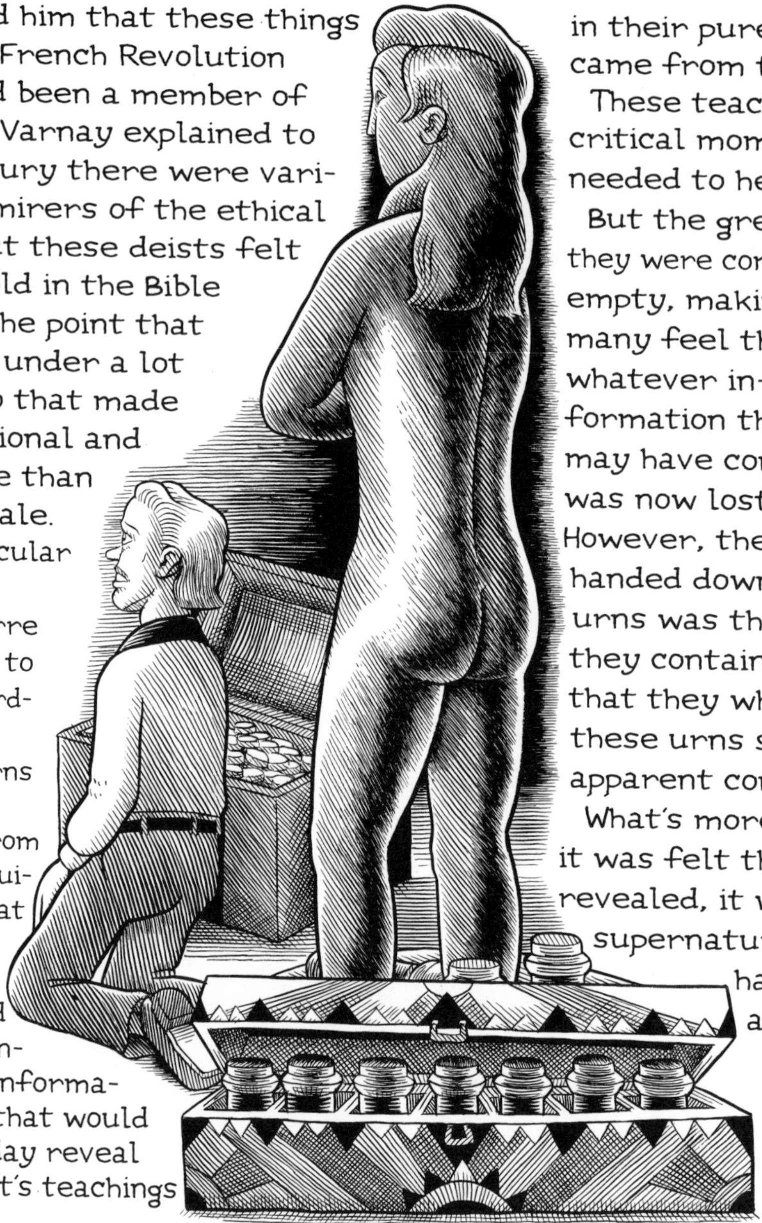

misguided affair, the urns disappeared and all memory of them became little more than a faint fable recalled by the very few.

The talking head instructed Varnay to use a portion of the gold he'd found to gather the urns and the strange statue into a place of safekeeping and told him that the true significance of these things would in time be revealed to him.

In the meantime, he was instructed to teach himself the ancient Greek and Hebrew languages and to keep his eye on breakthroughs in science that would be occurring in the next few years.

The first of these breakthroughs was Edison's discovery of recorded sound. In the year 1885, the head instructed him to attend a public demonstration of the phonograph.

Fully ten years later, he was told to attend the Lumière brothers' first demonstration of projected motion pictures.

By this time he was fluent in Hebrew and Greek. The head now told him that the next time he slept, he would have an instructive dream that would finally clear up much of the mystery that all the phenomena of those last few years had created in his mind. The prospect left him so excited that it was a full two days before he was able to sleep again. But sleep finally did come and with it, the promised dream.

In it he finds himself in the Holy Temple of Jerusalem, an apparently unseen witness to a major Biblical event!
For there before him, more vividly depicted than in any movie and yet strangely like one, he sees Jesus Christ, scourging the money changers, driving them from the Temple!
And off to one side, in a dark corner, there's a mysterious figure who he seems to instinctively realize is an Arab peddler, a nomad from a neighboring land,
who, even as his fellow merchants flee, hurries to finish what appears to be a glazing process scoring lines on a whirling urn
by means of a machine with a trundle operated by his feet,

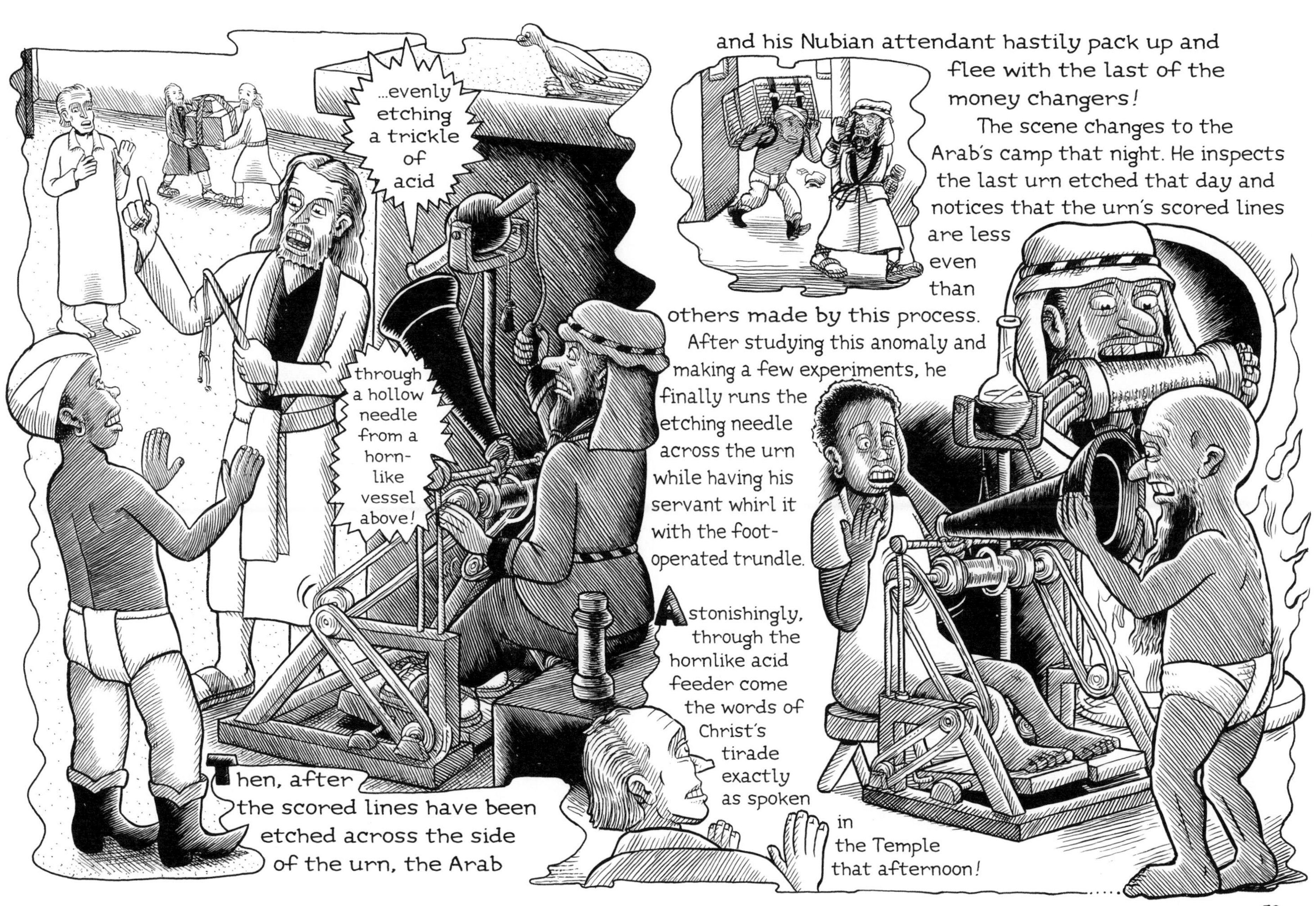

…evenly etching a trickle of acid
through a hollow needle from a horn-like vessel above!
Then, after the scored lines have been etched across the side of the urn, the Arab
and his Nubian attendant hastily pack up and flee with the last of the money changers!
The scene changes to the Arab's camp that night. He inspects the last urn etched that day and notices that the urn's scored lines are less even than others made by this process.
After studying this anomaly and making a few experiments, he finally runs the etching needle across the urn while having his servant whirl it with the foot-operated trundle.
Astonishingly, through the hornlike acid feeder come the words of Christ's tirade exactly as spoken in the Temple that afternoon!

Inadvertently, this merchant had stumbled upon the secret of recording the human voice nearly two thousand years before Edison's phonograph! Mr. Varnay told me he was no less thunderstruck by this revelation than the Arab merchant of long ago must have been.

The vision over, he obtained a cylinder phonograph and began to tinker with it.

After some days of trial and error, he finally got the strange urns to play. And this is where his acquired knowledge of Greek and Hebrew stood him in good stead.

Playing the seven urns as if they were cylinder recordings, he realized he had nothing less than the actual spoken words of Jesus Christ, incredibly and miraculously retrieved from the ancient past!

It was this message, Mr. Varnay told me, that he wanted to present to humanity. A message, he said, that the world sorely needed now, more than ever before.

Now Mr. Varnay opened a case next to the talking head that contained a custom-made phonograph and fixed the urn in place, just as though it were a cylinder record. The sound it produced was scratchy and quite faint, but by listening carefully, I heard what was a just barely recognizable voice.

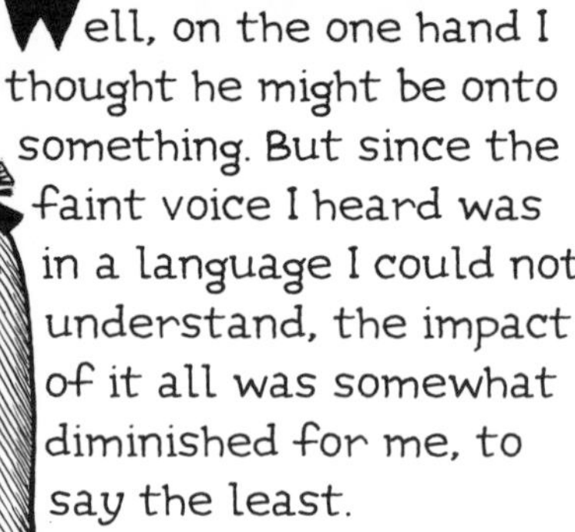

Well, on the one hand I thought he might be onto something. But since the faint voice I heard was in a language I could not understand, the impact of it all was somewhat diminished for me, to say the least.

Mr. Varnay seemed to understand this and flicked the machine off before it finished playing the urn. He walked around to the other side of the desk, put a sympathetic hand on my shoulder, and conceded that what he'd told me was a lot to take in all at once.

He suggested that I might like to rest awhile and that later, if I wished, we could drive to Irvington for a quiet dinner.

He led me to my room and bowed. Before going, he told me that the servants had been instructed that I was to have the run of the house and that my merest wish would be obeyed.

I was alone then, and it was all still feeling quite strange. But I was undeniably fascinated, really, almost to the point of giddiness.

I was way too keyed up to sleep, so I decided to take Mr. Varnay at his word and explore a little. I'd remembered seeing an impressive-looking grand piano in the main living room, and it was there that I found myself heading.

No servants were about, but Rousseau, who'd been napping in front of the fireplace, looked up curiously as I approached the piano.

I was enthralled by its tone as I tentatively fingered a Chopin étude.

I was astonished by the instrument's amazing resonance, though I gradually realized that what I heard was more than just the piano. That was when I looked and noticed that Rousseau was now sitting up next to me and whining along as I played, but in perfect harmonic pitch, adding an uncanny, lovely accompaniment to my playing.

I was both astonished and delighted. My playing grew in confidence and Rousseau kept up with me, complementing the music in a way I'd never dreamed possible! The dog had been so full of surprising novelty, and I couldn't imagine what could possibly happen to top this latest surprise, but something did. While what happened next was hardly earth-shaking, it was still quite a surprise. As I finished my remarkable duet with Rousseau, I heard Mr. Varnay compliment my performance. And as I turned toward him, I was quite surprised to see that he'd abandoned his 18th-century attire for a beautifully cut suit quite in tune with contemporary 20th-century fashion. It was not merely the unexpectedness of the change that surprised me, so much as how very splendid it made him look. Mr. Varnay may not have been exactly handsome in the conventional sense, but at the moment he looked remarkably attractive.

Noting my surprise, he explained that while he preferred 18th-century fashions, he did not often wear them in public, where it would bring undue attention to himself.

When we departed for the village a few minutes later, Weltman handed Mr. Varnay a very striking powder blue homburg hat,
...that enhanced his splendid appearance even further.
As we left for the waiting car, I was almost sorry when Mr. Varnay signaled to Rousseau not to follow.
However, the splendid beast seemed to take it in his stride as he turned and trotted back into the house.

My mind was in a delectable whirl as we approached the village. The late afternoon was just beginning to fade into evening as we passed the local nickelodeon theater. Posters out front proclaimed that the latest episode of Pearl White in "The Iron Claw" was playing, and there was quite a crowd waiting to get in.

All the exciting events of the day notwithstanding, I still felt a twinge of excitement in spite of myself. Maybe it was weakness, but I was still dying to know who The Laughing Mask was! I guess I was still a hopeless movie fan! Mr. Varnay noticed my interest

Chapter Six: Somewhere A Voice Is Calling

Well, the latest episode of "The Iron Claw" went over big with the crowd and with me, too.

And just as he'd done when he witnessed the last episode, in Lumberton, I noticed that Mr. Varnay was again making notes as he watched.

The feature was a film made by the famous woman director, Miss Lois Weber, and, like all of her interesting films, it had a story with a message, which in this case was about the evils of abortion. I found it rather moving, and while Mr. Varnay had put away his notebook, he too was following it with interest.

Afterwards, his driver, Lionel, dropped us off at a charming Italian restaurant – nothing fancy, but wonderful atmosphere.

Later, as we lingered over a small bottle of chianti, Mr. Varnay asked me how I liked the show. I told him I'd been a huge fan of Pearl White ever since "The Perils of Pauline." Mr. Varnay said he shared my admiration for Pearl White's films and mentioned, to my surprise, that he was slightly acquainted with her.

Well, at least he wasn't blowing about what great pals they were, like Abe Fortune. What he did tell me was that Molly O'Dare's company wasn't the first film studio he'd worked for. He told me he'd also worked for the Wharton brothers in Ithaca, New York, where Pearl White's last serials had been produced and that he'd been initially hoping to interest her in working on a film project he had in mind.

When I asked him what happened, he tactfully avoided answering and mentioned that he was planning to make a serial film of his own, with the idea of using it as a vehicle to tell the world about his discovery of the seven urns with the recordings of Christ's voice.

Then he asked me what I thought of the feature we'd seen that had been made by Lois Weber.* I said I liked it and had been a fan of hers for several years, going back to the days when she starred in them herself.

Where Are My Children? 1916

This seemed to interest him and he cited her as a prime example of his theory that women, at their best, were essentially more highly evolved in terms of human progress than men were. He told me that Lois Weber's approach to filmmaking as a kind of secular ministry, with her films themselves being sermons that stood a greater chance of reaching the public than the ones they heard in church, had greatly inspired him.

Pouring a little more wine in my glass, he asked me if I'd seen her film "The Hypocrites." Well, I certainly had. "The Hypocrites" featured a naked woman in it, billed as The Naked Truth, who wandered though the film exposing different situations of hypocrisy. It was a smash hit in Lumberton and played there for weeks, although, I'm afraid, for all the wrong reasons. Still, I had been greatly taken with its striking attack on the hypocrisy of mankind.

The Hypocrites, 1915

You can well imagine that I was pretty eager by this time to hear more about Mr. Varnay's project, but instead, he felt the need to explain further the significance of the urns.

Well, that was true. Outside a certain novelty involved, I had to admit, it all seemed rather remote and confusing to me.

Mr. Varnay explained that what was so striking

*Lois Weber: Active as an actress and director of films in the teens and early 1920s, usually with a muckraking or messianic message in their storyline.

Lois Weber

about the urns, when listened to and fully absorbed, was the way they tended to demystify Christ's message to the world. He told me that the desire of many deist groups to get rid of what they perceived as tacked-on supernatural stuff in the Bible had been quite prevalent during the 18th-century Age of Enlightenment. He said even the American President, Thomas Jefferson, had been highly influenced by such thinking and had gone so far as to make his own Bible by editing out everything in the four gospels of Jesus Christ that struck him as spurious and most likely to have been added later for various reasons by other hands. Jefferson felt that, when these parts were edited from the story, what remained was the most excellent guide to human ethical behavior that our world had yet been given.

However, Mr. Varnay said that the spoken voice on the urns went much further than the Jefferson Bible. He told me that Christ's spoken message did not deny the possibility of heaven, but seemed to imply that humanity, over time, would evolve to higher levels and one day make its own heaven right here on earth. And that as people did evolve, they would, in time, even grasp the real key to immortality, which, Mr. Varnay serenely informed me, had to do with a kind of reincarnation that he felt wasn't really such a mystical idea, but more likely an aspect of science that humanity had not yet caught up with.

I had to admit there was something striking in all of this, particularly the part about reincarnation. And I readily confessed that I occasionally had feelings that I might have lived before.

Mr. Varnay grabbed my hand, saying,

Oh my! I'm not sure I believed him, but it all seemed very romantic to me, especially after three glasses of wine, and it struck me then that perhaps he really did mean for us to be lovers.

But Varnay quickly threw cold water on my wine-induced reverie. He told me that he was certain we had been lovers, once upon a time, and would perhaps be so again, but not in this lifetime.

He told me that the males of the human species needed to catch up with the more highly evolved females; this could, in fact, be sped up through a careful program of eugenic* breeding in much the same way that he had managed to breed the remarkably advanced Rousseau.

In him you see the proof of this!

Well, maybe. But, I've got to say, Ellie, once again it was all starting to feel a bit over my head and strange! Mr. Varnay seemed to sense this because once again he seemed to rein himself in.

Come, we've talked enough of such heavy subjects for one night!

But as we were leaving, he dropped one final conversational bomb, which was that I shouldn't despair of ever finding a mate and that part of his mission was to seek out a suitable, evolved man for me to marry and mate with.

I didn't say it to his face, but the idea that he wanted to breed me like a dog didn't really appeal to me, and I was stewing over it on the ride back to the house.

*Eugenic breeding: The so-called science of improving evolving species through selective breeding.

But when Rousseau gave us a barky welcome our return, all of that flew out of my mind, and I didn't need to be coaxed when Mr. Varnay asked me if I'd favor him with some more music.
I was about to play another Chopin thing when I noticed the sheet music for the song "Somewhere A Voice Is Calling" sitting on the piano.
I'd always loved John McCormack's* haunting record of that song and quite spontaneously, I began to play and sing it.
Dusk and the shadows fa-lling, O'er land and sea somewhere a voice is calling, ca-lling for me...
Again Rousseau joined in with his eerily apt doggy harmonics, but before I'd gotten much further
in the song, another voice joined us. It was Mr. Varnay, singing in a most pleasing light baritone.
To say that I was enchanted by this scarcely does the moment justice. While it may not have been strictly true, at that moment, I felt thoroughly convinced that even John McCormack himself would have been impressed by our spontaneous rendition of that gorgeous song!
* John McCormack: an Irish singer of the period, arguably one of the greatest singers of all time.

THE MARCH OF HUMANITY
In six stages
1
2
3
4
5
6
Later, as I lay in bed, my mind dizzily whirled as all the incredible incidents of the last few days swirled before me. It was all quite strange, to say the least! But for all that,
Somewhere a voice is calling, ca-lling for me
...it had been a truly wonderful day!

Chapter Seven: The Goddess of Enlightenment

Needless to say, I didn't sleep very well. In fact, I woke up suddenly just before dawn.

In my dream, I'd been hearing two people talking in what sounded like French, but now that I was awake, I realized it wasn't a dream, for I could still hear a faint, steady stream of conversation in French.

Clearly it was none of my affair, but in spite of myself, I felt a strong urge to investigate. Throwing on a robe, I went out into the hall and could now hear that the voices were coming from a room at the other end of it.

I was somewhat shocked at my own audacity, but I quietly tried the door, which was unlocked.

As the first shards of morning light came through the room's window, I beheld a most unusual sight.

There was Mr. Varnay, in his night shirt, in front of the talking head! Rousseau sat next to him and noticed me as I stood watching. For a moment I was afraid he might attack, but instead he walked over to me and licked my hand. Emboldened by this, I entered the room until I was standing right over Mr. Varnay, who took no notice of me as I studied him more closely.

The head's mouth was moving in sync with a sonorous voice that I could see was actually coming from Mr. Varnay, because his lips moved slightly as

the head spoke. In Mr. Varnay's lap was a book, in which he seemed to be taking down everything the head was saying. Occasionally he seemed to ask a question in his normal voice, but also in French, and he seemed to be in a strong trance.

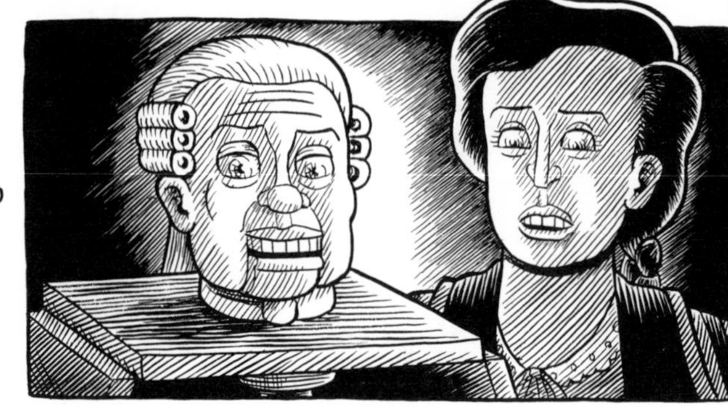

I went over to the head and more closely observed it. I could detect no string or any visible device causing its mouth to move. It was all very strange and, but for Mr. Varnay's description of what I'd just seen the day before, I might have reacted more in panic at the sight of all this than I did. Instead I stayed and observed for another minute and then returned to my room.

Later, at breakfast, Mr. Varnay seemed quite chipper. If he'd seen me in his room earlier, he betrayed absolutely no evidence of it now. He did tell me that that morning, he'd been working on a screenplay he wanted to produce and held up the very large notebook I saw him taking dictation in earlier. He told me he'd like to read some of it to me after breakfast if I cared to hear it.

I said I would as calmly as possible because, Ellie, at that point I was dying to hear it!

Shortly thereafter, we convened in the same study we were in the day before, although this time he pointedly did not lock the door.

In essence, he told me he wanted to produce a serial film called "The Goddess of Enlightenment," and he wanted me to star in it! Before I could respond,

he quickly added that this would in no way occur in the sordid kind of atmosphere that I had encountered with Molly O'Dare's film crew.

He told me that he had seen similar unwholesome environments in the various other studios he'd worked in and was also generally disappointed by the behavior of various female players he'd observed in his ongoing search for a woman to star in his own production. He told me he'd actually been on the verge of giving the whole thing up when he saw me in Lumberton. Not only did I seem to be the sort of high-minded person he was looking for, but,

You've seen for yourself your astonishing resemblance to the statue I discovered!

He told me that seeing me naked confirmed his certainty that I was indeed the one.

He explained to me that his choice of a film to spread his message was because of their overwhelming popularity throughout the world. Then he told me another reason he wanted to see me undressed was because he wanted me to appear nude in several scenes of the film.

Well! That may have explained why he'd asked me to take my clothes off, but it also struck me as a direct contradiction to all this high-minded stuff he'd been going on about! He seemed to anticipate me, telling me he had several reasons for this. For one thing, he pointed out that nudity in films was coming to be accepted by most local censors, provided that it was done tastefully. Again he cited Lois Weber's production "The Hypocrites" as an example. He also showed me an ad in a film trade magazine showing an advertisement for a new film starring a famous artist's model named Audrey Munson.* This was to be the second movie in which Miss Munson would appear in the nude.

Inspiration, 1915, with Audrey Munson.

Indeed, I remember the first one, "Inspiration," which had been a big hit in Lumberton. I told Mr. Varnay that I'd seen it and while I conceded that the film wasn't lurid per se, it was also true that the reason we did good business with it had everything to do with its nude scenes.

You just made my second point,

said Mr. Varnay. He told me that another motivation for having nude scenes was to attract a larger audience who might most benefit from the film's actual message.

*Audrey Munson: A well-known artist's model who appeared in four films. She lived fast and died at age 100 as an inmate in a New York state insane asylum.

Warming to the subject, he said the great tragedy of Christianity, in the various sects that it exists in today, is the way it is so willfully warped and twisted to fit the agendas of various seats of power in the world.

How else could we have a war taking place in Europe right now in which all sides claim that Jesus Christ is on their side?

Everyone praises Christ's teachings and yet hardly anyone follows them!

But, if the world could be made truly aware of his pure, unadulterated teachings, in his own voice, it could be a major step toward making this world a better place.

It was a lot to take in, but I was undeniably intrigued to hear the story he wanted to tell me.

Editor's note:

While nothing but a few fragments of film from "The Goddess of Enlightenment" seem to exist today, I have reconstructed it, in the scenes that follow and elsewhere in this story, from Katherine Whaley's descriptions and from production stills found by Eleanor Whaley and loaned to me during the making of this book. -K.D.

One final tidbit of information he mentioned before starting to read was that he hired Allen Rollins to be my leading man. He told me that Rollins deeply regretted the accident that occurred at the Lumberton sawmill when he was with the Molly O'Dare crew. He went on to say that

Well, I certainly hoped so! And with that, he launched into the story.

The opening scene takes place on the outskirts of a Roman town, some years after the crucifixion of Christ.

A nomadic Arab, a former follower of Christ and keeper of seven sacred urns having some secret connection with Christ, has somehow fallen out with Christ's other remaining disciples.

This Arab, now elderly, has formed his own splinter group of Christians

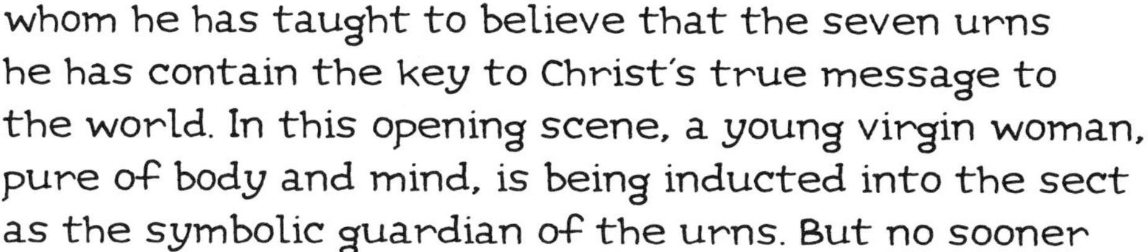

whom he has taught to believe that the seven urns he has contain the key to Christ's true message to the world. In this opening scene, a young virgin woman, pure of body and mind, is being inducted into the sect as the symbolic guardian of the urns. But no sooner have they concluded the ceremony when trouble strikes!

A squad of thugs, representing another Christian group, charges into the tent and cuts down everyone in sight!

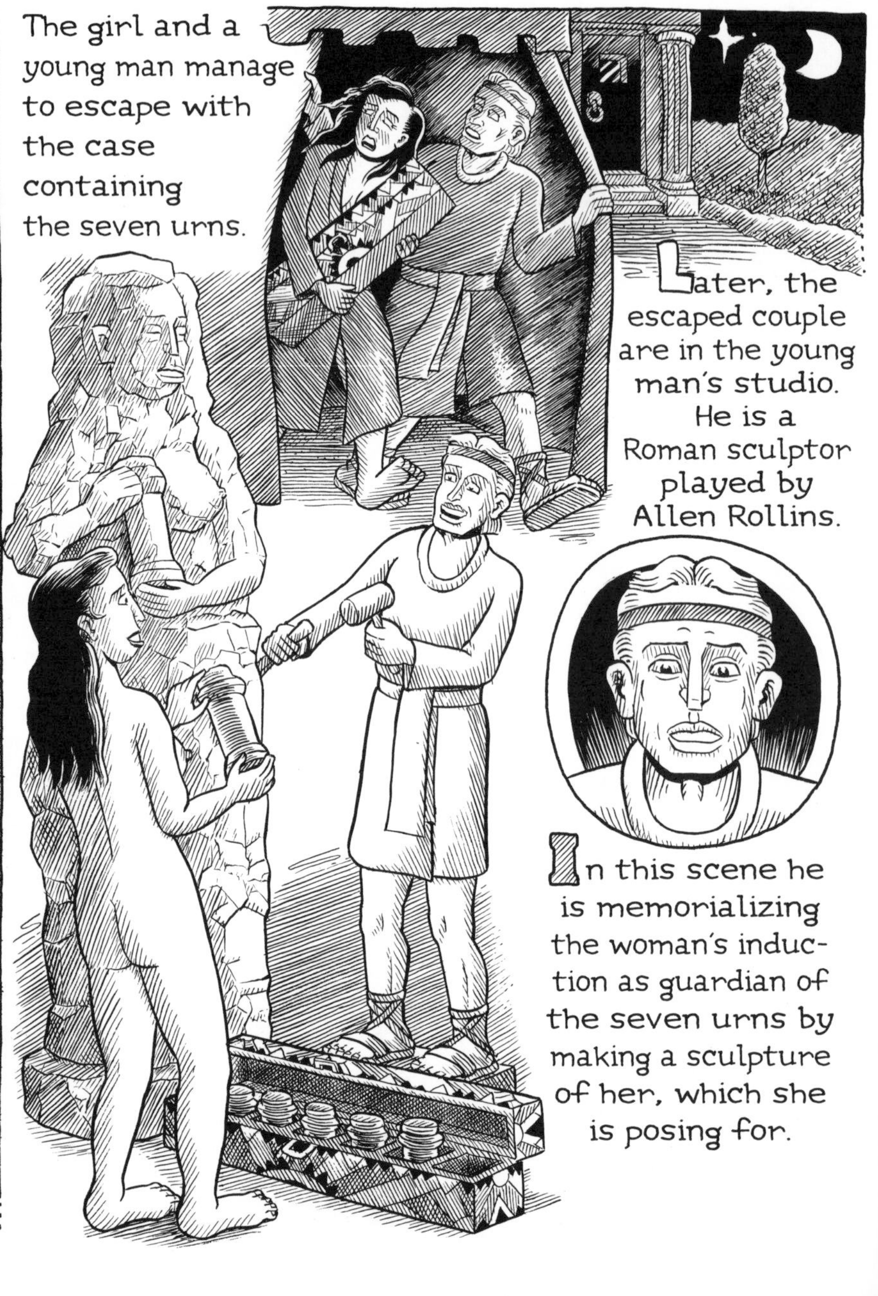

The girl and a young man manage to escape with the case containing the seven urns.

Later, the escaped couple are in the young man's studio. He is a Roman sculptor played by Allen Rollins.

In this scene he is memorializing the woman's induction as guardian of the seven urns by making a sculpture of her, which she is posing for.

A few days later, the young man is spotted in the streets of Rome and pointed out as a Christian heretic by the same men who took part in the slaughter.
When the Roman authorities try to get him to betray the girl and give up the urns, he refuses. And a few days later,
he's brutally executed.

Robespierre is not really in the cult's inner circle. He knows about the seven urns, but like most cult members he does not truly understand their significance, only that when their secret is revealed, it will line up perfectly with the rational laws of natural science.

This rationality appeals to Robespierre's modern deist mentality.

As they leave the meeting, the young noble wears the cap of a revolutionary French citizen, so Robespierre seems to be involved in keeping the young man's noble rank a secret.

On the street they witness the arrest of a young French noblewoman. She is an exact double of the girl guardian of the seven urns shown in the previous scenes!

The disguised noble reacts in shock at the sight of this arrest and implores Robespierre...
...to use his influence to save the woman!
Robespierre balks at this until the noble pulls him back into a secret inner room.
In this room is the Roman nude statue!
When Robespierre sees it, he is astonished at its spitting likeness to the young noblewoman whose arrest they just witnessed!
Later, after Robespierre somehow obtains her release,

in a scene involving Mesmerism, the rescued Noblewoman begins to recall a secret of the past that begins to explain how the urns and the statue ended up in France. She is even about to explain how the urns actually work when a mob of French citizens raid the meeting!

In short order the young nobleman, the woman and others at the meeting, including Robespierre, are captured and charged, although the urns and statue are not found.

But all the captured deists are summarily sentenced to death!

Episode one ends with them riding in a wagon to the guillotine!

Well, quirkily, unlike most serial cliffhangers I'd ever seen, they were all executed!
I started to say something, but Mr. Varnay held up his hand and smiled.
Wait,
he said.
Well, the scene changes from 18th-century France to the France of a hundred years later.
The statue, the urns and a fortune in gold are found in the basement bunker that lay beneath the house in the last episode, long since demolished!
The young man who discovers all this is a direct descendant of the executed French nobleman and is again played by Allen Rollins.
This fictional character was loosely based on Mr. Varnay himself.
Among all the exotic booty, the young man finds a note telling him that the reincarnated soul of the girl who posed for the statue known as The Goddess of Enlightenment will be found in the United States.
He is instructed to go there and find her.

Through her, he is told, he will find out the secret of the seven urns!
Some time later, on the voyage to America, he sees an American girl on the ship who is an exact double of the
Goddess of Enlightenment!
He approaches and asks for a dance.
As they glide along, she is warm and friendly.
But when he begins to tell her of his quest, she smiles and puts a finger to her lips.
Suddenly there's a huge disruption!
A strange group of masked men enter the ballroom!

They seize the girl!
And take her and the statue into a strange submarine that has mysteriously appeared alongside the ship!
With their plunder in hand and the boarding ladder of the odd craft folded back into itself, the mysterious men sink into the vast ocean from which they came! Which is how episode two ended!
By this time I was absolutely crazy to hear episode three, and Mr. Varnay did not disappoint me!

In episode three the young man has arrived in America. He is utterly dejected to have been so close to his objective, only to have it so mysteriously snatched away.
While trying to drown his troubles in drink in a low dive, he is shocked to see the abducted girl entertaining there!
But when, in his drunken frenzy, he tries to approach her, she reacts scornfully!
She tells him she's never been to Europe and has
. . . never before laid eyes on him in all her life!
Later, on the edge of despair, he decides to end it all.
But as he hits the water, a motor boat appears!
A mysterious masked stranger pulls him into the boat!
He looks and is dressed exactly like the leader of the men who abducted the girl in episode 2!
When the young man struggles, the stranger knocks him out!

Later, he awakens in a dingy waterfront hotel room with a sore jaw and a note pinned to his shirt!
The note says,
Take heart. The girl you saw last night is the girl you seek. But there is danger about, which is why she pretended not to know you. All will be well. But you must guard the sacred urns with your life! A Friend
At this point I was loving the story. It was every bit as good as "The Iron Claw" as far as I was concerned, and I eagerly demanded to know what happened next. Mr. Varnay smiled somewhat apologetically, shrugged, and told me that was as far as he'd gotten so far.
But he was immensely pleased with my response, as his idea was to get every movie fan in the world on the edge of their seats, wanting to know the secret of the seven urns
Well! If I was anything to go by, he was heading in the right direction!

Chapter Eight: Follow The Dog

The next day was full of excitement as we took the train into New York City.

Mr. Varnay had rented a studio to take some photos of Allen Rollins and myself.

What was especially exciting to me was that this was my first sight of fabulous New York City. And I must say, even before we got out of Grand Central Station, I was utterly astounded!

Seeing Grand Central, which was nothing less than a complete underground town all by itself, absolutely amazed me!

In the photography studio, Mr. Varnay had the original of the statue I'd seen a copy of in Lumberton.

I soon discovered that other than some makeup and some hair styling, no costume was needed for me. I was somewhat alarmed to find out that I was expected to be quite naked in these shots! But as the others seemed to be all poised for business, I put my best bare foot forward.
To my immense relief, Allen Rollins and the photographer, who seemed to be a friend of Allen's, conducted themselves
in an entirely courteous and professional manner, though I was rather surprised when an hour or so into the session
PICK A STAR!

I saw the photographer and Allen kissing while we were on a break! Observing
their demeanor together more closely, I soon began to realize that these two were something *more* than friends!
I'll admit that I was initially somewhat shocked by this. Of course, I knew of such things, but this was my first real exposure to it. Mr. Varnay, however, seemed to take it in his stride.
Later, he explained to me that many actors on the stage and in movies were homosexuals and that in

many ways this often worked out rather well. He told me that I'd most likely be seeing a good deal of Allen and I wouldn't have to be constantly on edge, worrying that he might be trying to involve me in some sexual escapade.

I had to admit, on reflection, that he had a point and it also

gave me hope once again that something romantic might yet develop between Mr. Varnay and myself.

The next day, he took me along when Lionel drove him out to Matesak, New Jersey, where the film studio Mr. Varnay had purchased was located. The studio had recently been owned by a European refugee named Malek Janochek

...who had been filming an ill-fated serial there called "Alias The Cat,"* which featured both himself and Molly O'Dare. Janochek, who'd been leading a strange double life, had ultimately experienced a huge disaster during the filming that resulted in his own untimely death and a disastrous fire

* See Alias The Cat, Stuff of Dreams #2 Fantagraphics

that burned a good deal of the Non Pareil studio.

But apparently the damage to the studio was more superficial than was first reported, which I soon saw for myself as Mr. Varnay took me through the place.

In fact, Mr. Varnay said he'd gotten a rather good bargain and felt the expense of getting it up and running would be fairly nominal.

I could also sense, as we looked at the surviving scenery and other remnants of Janochek's ill-starred venture, that it wasn't just the fact that the studio was a good bargain that had attracted Mr. Varnay to this place. He told me that while many of Janochek's misguided dealings were apparently unlawful, he still admired his motives.

I could feel that all of this morose talk of Janochek had gotten Mr. Varnay into a somewhat melancholy mood. And in an attempt to snap him out of it, I told him how much I'd enjoyed what he had told me of the serial's story so far and how eager I was to hear more.

It was then that I discovered that it was more than being in Janochek's shadow that had him down. Mr Varnay then admitted to me that he was kind of stuck about where the Goddess of Enlightenment story was going next. He explained to me that he knew where it had to end up, which was revealing a more secular and scientifically plausible message of Jesus Christ, but that coming up with all of the myriad details of such a wildly exciting story that the public would get hooked on, hooked on so much that they'd soak up the film's real message before they even realized they'd done so, well, much of that, he confessed, still eluded him.

Well, that was troubling, but then something occurred to me and it came tumbling out of my mouth before I even realized it.

Of course! ROUSSEAU!
A second later he lifted me up and whirled me around, kissing me on both cheeks.
And all the way home he was ebulliently full of the idea – *my* idea!
Weltman eyed us suspiciously as we danced into the house, supposing, I guess, that we were drunk, and I guess, in a way, we were, though on nothing so crude as liquor.
Mr. Varnay was elated
and I was supremely happy to be sharing the moment and very proud, indeed, that I had contributed to it.

We all had a good sing before going to bed.

Well, the next morning, Mr. Varnay informed me that he had more story he wanted to read to me and even encouraged Rousseau to come with us while he did so.

Episode four, called "Follow The Dog,"

picks up with the young man waking up in a strange hotel room, reading the note instructing him to guard the seven urns with his life.
Unfortunately, he's pawned them to drown his woes in drink. And now he has no money to redeem the pawn ticket!
Suddenly he hears barking just outside his door!
Arf! Arf!
It is Rousseau!
He has a bundle tied to a stick, which he drops at the young man's feet. There's a note pinned to the bundle which says,
There is money enough in this bundle to redeem the pawn ticket in your possession. Just follow the dog. But when you do so, use the things in this bundle to disguise yourself. You are being watched. Beware! A. Friend.

The articles of clothing in the bundle give him the appearance of a blind beggar,

BLIND

...and soon he's out on the street in this disguise.

The BLACK MACAW

POOR PETER'S

BLIND

He redeems the urns in the shop where he pawned them,

BLIND

ISAAC & SON

ISAAC

CASH FOR GOLD

...and many pairs of suspicious, sullen eyes observe him,

BLIND

...as he again follows the dog down several crooked side streets of the water-front town!

MUSEUM of NATURAL ENLIGHTENMENT
Truth Will Set You Free!
MISSING LINKS
NEW REVELATIONS
CLOSED
DR. GERMAINE SAINT PIERRE PROPRIETOR
BLIND
LET THERE BE ENLIGHTENMENT

Finally they approach what appears to be some sort of dime museum.

He is beckoned to enter by the proprietor

...Who is played by Mr. Varnay.

CLOSED
DR. GERMAINE SAINT PIERRE PROPRIETOR
By Appointment Only

The proprietor pats the dog, who clearly knows him.

The young man feels a glimmering of recognition!

...and a growing certainty that he's seen this Dr. Saint Pierre before!

The proprietor tries to assure him that all is well, but he's only marginally successful.

Then he opens his coat and the young man immediately recognizes the odd, militaristic uniform he wears!

And he now realizes that this is the man who led the squad that abducted the girl, and the statue, and who also prevented the young man's earlier suicide attempt!

The urns are unwrapped and placed behind the ticket booth.
The Knights of Enlightenment ..... seven men and a dog.
There's a stage with six military figures stiffly posed in a kind of sword salute.
He recognizes them as the men who abducted the girl and the statue. Rousseau stands in front of them looking quite jaunty and military himself. Flanking either side of them are two draped objects that have ropes tied to their tops.
THE BOOK OF Enlightenment!
Enlightenment!
Then the young man is invited to follow the museum proprietor to the back to witness a presentation especially for his benefit.
Soon to be eight men, a dog and one young lady.

Next, he pulls the rope, which lifts the draping on one flanking object, revealing the statue, telling the young man as he does so, that the statue depicts the Goddess of Enlightenment, symbolic guardian of the seven sacred urns.
Then he pulls the other rope and there, in the same pose, is the girl!
"And this," he says, "is Katherine, the Goddess of Enlightenment".
The girl smiles,
...and after being helped into a robe, she is introduced to the young man.

He's then led toward an imposing book near-by.

The girl seems amused by the look of consternation on the young man's face.

Unable to contain himself any longer, he suddenly exclaims,

"You!"

"Yes," declares the stranger. "You two *have* met before, but *just* not recently, as you seem to believe."

He opens the book to an illustration of the induction of the Goddess of Enlightenment in ancient times ex-actly as depicted in the serial's first episode!

Subsequent pages show other moments including
The induction breaking up!
The young Roman carving the statue!
The 18th-century girl beginning to explain the meaning of the urns!
Then the girl and the young nobleman on their way to execution!
And finally, a picture of the young man himself discovering the urns, the statue and the gold!

It is then that the stranger tells the young man that he and she are the living reincarnated spirits of these same two people, destined to play a major role in steering the world away from impending disaster.

In back, one of the six knights is discovered still in the smart salute pose!
He is discovered to be a dummy dressed in the uniform of one of the knights!
There is a traitor among them, which is where episode Four ends!
I *loved* it! And, of course, I was thrilled that it was *my* suggestion that got the scenario back on track!

In fact, from that point on, Mr. Varnay relied on me frequently for story ideas, which I believe was something that brought us closer together although, alas, still not as close as I hoped we one day might be.

One curious thing happened at about this time, though, which *did* seem like life imitating art. Weltman was caught by Rousseau in the act of robbing the house of every conceivably pawnable item in the house, including the urns!

Because of the sheer volume of the items he was caught with, Mr. Varnay concluded that the urns were probably not the focus of the robbery, and Mr. Varnay did not mention them in the report he made to the Irvington Police when he pressed charges against Weltman.

It did, however, bring an abrupt end to our Irvington household.

After that, Mr. Varnay set me up in a Manhattan apartment in Gramercy Park, a relatively quiet neighborhood

and yet only a stone's throw from bustling Union Square on Fourteenth Street. He retained Marie to keep house for me, and he and I shared Lionel, who split his time chauffeuring me and driving Mr. Varnay about in Matesak, New Jersey, where Mr. Varnay had set up camp in the Non Pareil film studio while busily getting it back in working order.
To keep me occupied while all this was going on, he'd engaged a tutor to begin my further education, which he decided would commence with my learning the French language.
Not that there wasn't plenty to keep me occupied, because he'd already begun a publicity campaign for "The Goddess of Enlightenment," even though not a foot of film had yet been shot.
Mr. Larry Lippman, post graduate French Studies, Columbia University.
Photographs that he'd had taken of Allen Rollins and myself were already running in advertisements he'd placed in various movie trade magazines,
so I'd already achieved a small degree of fame. Of course it might have also been called notoriety, since most of these ads featured me in the nude!
Although as Mr. Varnay pointed out time and again, there was nothing at all trashy in any of this!
74
At Last!
A thrilling chapter play that will UNCOVER the NAKED TRUTH of VITAL concern to ALL the beings of our World!
Introducing Miss Katherine Whaley
The Goddess of Enlightenment
Moving Picture World
75
To The Public! While much in our story is daringly frank and uncompromising, be assured that nothing in the way of vulgar exploitation will be seen in this photoplay. Charles Andreas Varnay
And, along with these ads, he gave out many interviews that always stressed the intrinsic high-mindedness of the production.

In contrast to my nakedness in the advertising, he went out of his way to see that I was the best dressed woman in New York City, spending lavishly on my wardrobe.
CHICK
He had me "seen" thus attired, in all the "best places," usually in the company of Allen Rollins. In fact, even when Mr. Varnay was with us, he always went out of his way to make it appear that I was actually Allen's date. This was, he told me, because it would be good publicity if it could be made to seem as if there were some kind of romance going on between Allen and me.
ALLEN
There!
Of course, everywhere we went, Chick, Allen's boyfriend, was close at hand and at work photographing us in any situations the press at large may have missed.

Surprise snack time at the zoo!
The wild winds of 23rd St. out in front of the "Flatiron" building!
Somewhere a voice is calling
John McCormack in concert at the massive New York Hippodrome.
And the fact is, I soon became reasonably fond of both of them. They were fun to be with and knew all about how to have a good time in New York City.
Riding in Central Park!

Allen began to teach me to dance, because dancing was something he especially excelled at.
REISENWEBERS
Felton's Cafe
Felton's
Happy's Hottentot Novelty JASS BAND
One night we went over to Felton's café over on Columbus Circle to hear and dance to the new jazz music, which I thought was rather funny, but fun to dance to.
Allen told me I'd really missed the great dancing days in New York City, which he told me had flourished in a series of dance clubs run by Vernon and Irene Castle
Happy's Hottentot NOVELTY JASS BAND

from 1913 to late in 1915 when Vernon, being English, had retired from dancing to become an aviator to fight for his native land in the big European war.

Allen told me he'd gotten his start in show business as a dance instructor in one of the Castles' clubs, an establishment called Castles By The Sea that ran for about six months during the spring and summer of 1915 at Coney Island.

He told me there was still one place in the city where you could see good dancing. This was a club in Harlem called The Tempo Club, where one could listen and dance to the Jim Europe band.

James Reese Europe had been the dance director for the Castles at all their clubs and on their tours. Of course I'd heard of Jim Europe. Being a negro, his sponsorship by the Castles had been rather controversial. What Allen said about that was, his being black was actually a plus, as negroes tended to have a superior sense of rhythm when it came to things musical.

I had a chance to find out for myself the next night and, indeed, I couldn't help but feel that Allen was onto something. While the Europe band had a similar rhythm to the combo at Felton's, they were, at the same time, more melodic and generally more refined, altogether ideal for dancing. What's more, when Allen introduced me to James Europe, I found him to very congenial, articulate and, like his music, rather refined.

It was also interesting hearing Allen and Chick reminisce with him about the old days and also what the Castles were now doing. Europe told Allen that Vernon had gotten his flying license and was ready to do whatever it was going to take to get into the air on the allied side.

I was flattered when Mr. Europe said that he'd heard of me. While he clearly must have seen some of the nude photos of me that were in circulation, he made no snide remarks about it, which I occasionally got from some people at that time.

He told me that Irene Castle was now at work doing something similar to what I was doing. She was currently filming a serial called "Patria," which was being filmed by the Wharton brothers in Ithaca, New York. The serial was being bankrolled by the newspaper tycoon William Randolph Hearst, and was characterized as what was then being called a "preparedness film," essentially trading on the current and ultimately correct conventional wisdom that America too would soon be actually involved in the European War.

This was the view that Jim Europe also seemed to subscribe to,

as he somberly informed us that he was planning to enlist himself to be ready to fight just as soon as America got into it.

Well, the pall of gloom from all that war talk was soon broken in a surprising way. Apparently a dance contest was about to begin, and Mr. Europe excused himself to get the music for it started.

Allen nudged me, saying,

Now you're going to see some real dancing.

And sure enough, out of the wings, one couple at a time emerged dancing to a song Allen told me was a European classic called "Too Much Mustard."

Allen was right! As one couple after another, all negroes, emerged, the dancing was extraordinary! But the biggest surprise of all was when the last couple emerged. There on the floor of the Tempo Club, dancing magnificently, were Marie and her husband, Lionel.

When I whispered – well, with all the music, I guess I must've shouted – that Marie was my maid and Lionel was my chauffeur, Allen and Chick laughed with delight, and I must say I felt a good deal of pride rooting for them as they competed in the contest. After six numbers and as many different dances, I cheered lustily when they took the prize.

They seemed chagrined when they finally saw me, but that quickly dispelled when they saw how entertained I was by it all. It certainly created a stronger bond, not only between them and me, but also with Allen and Chick.

Chapter Nine

Meanwhile, Mr. Varnay's work getting the Non Pareil studio in shape progressed. In late September he had it ready, and I assumed that meant we'd soon begin shooting, since Mr. Varnay and myself had pretty well worked out all the action business of the story. However, he told me that he still needed to iron out aspects of the story's philosophical content.

He told me he planned to work on this during a trip to Europe he was making to arrange European distribution of the film. Naturally, with all the talk of war, this worried me. Already several American ships had been torpedoed crossing the Atlantic.

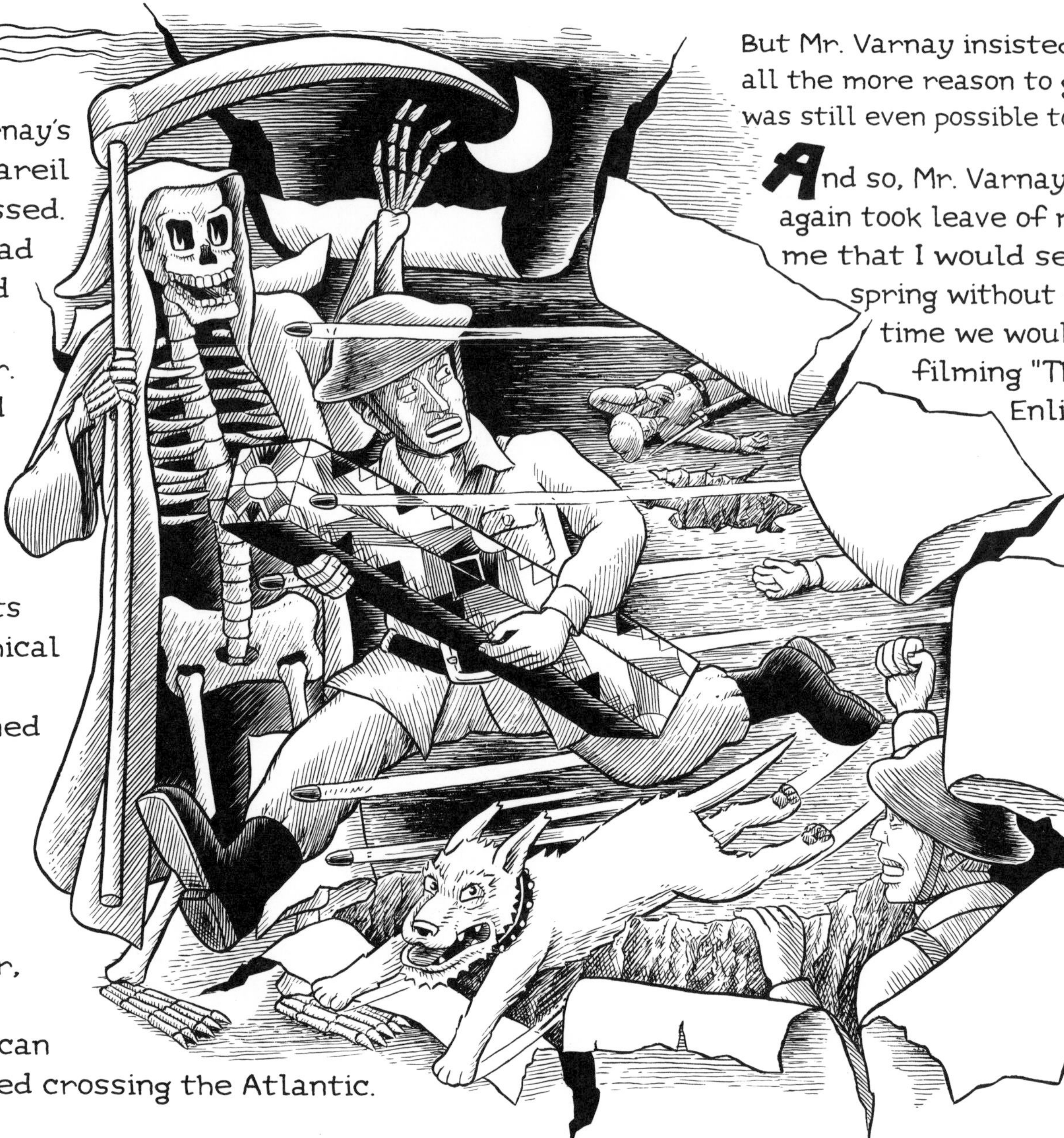

But Mr. Varnay insisted that this was all the more reason to go now, while it was still even possible to make the trip.

And so, Mr. Varnay and Rousseau again took leave of me. He assured me that I would see them next spring without fail, at which time we would commence filming "The Goddess of Enlightenment."

Well, of course, I missed Mr. Varnay and Rousseau, but I must say Allen, Chick, Marie and Lionel did everything in their power to keep me from being lonely.

Mr. Varnay had left a pile of books on various philosophical subjects that he wanted me to read during his absence,
VOLTAIRE
KANT
PLATO
DARWIN
CARLISLE
JEFFERSON
ARISTOTLE
but I must confess, I was having entirely too much fun to give them more than a glance.
AN IMPROMPTU DANCE LESSON AT THE KIT KAT CLUB.
MON HOMME
However, Marie helped me with my French homework and, little by little, both of us were becoming fairly adept at speaking and reading that language—
French ~ English
COLLETTE
good enough, in any event, to get through some pretty racy French novels. (with a bit of help from a dictionary...)
AT A PRIVATE CLUB IN GREENWICH VILLAGE, THE POODLE DOODLE.
And I'm afraid those were the only books I read while Mr. Varnay was absent!

1916
SUMMER
FUN.
Oh I hate to see that evenin sun go down!

I met some other men and perhaps flirted with one or two. But I was having too much fun to complicate things that way. Besides, for all of it, and it was glorious, I missed Mr. Varnay! And one thing that did worry me was the fact that I did not receive a single letter from him during his absence.
Keep the home-fires burning
Well, all good things must come to an end and ours ended rather abruptly early in 1917 when Jim Europe, as good as his word, quit the Tempo Club, disbanded his orchestra and enlisted! If that wasn't bad enough, Lionel followed Europe's example and enlisted too!
COLETTE

Mr. Varnay and Rousseau returned the next spring looking quite bright-eyed and bushy-tailed respectively. There was a new mood in the air. It was beyond preparedness and more like war fever.
In spite of it or maybe even trading on its energy, Mr. Varnay got right to work on "The Goddess of Enlightenment." The studio hummed with activity.
Location stuff at the Brooklyn Bridge.
And so it went all through spring and into the summer.

By that time, America was officially in the war and we soon worked it into the storyline.
By the end of Summer, Lionel had gotten through basic training and was now fighting somewhere in France. His occasional letters, which were quite moving, were read to me by Marie.
FORWARD
STOP
REVERSE
Life was hectic and more uncertain, but we were working hard and I was still very happy.
From Episode 6, Canine Courageous

But as worn out as I was by the end of the summer, I was surprised and disappointed too, when at about the half way point in the production, Mr. Varnay told me he was closing the studio until next spring while he and Rousseau took a trip to Los Angeles.

He told me there was an excellent opportunity for Rousseau to get a good part in a movie being made by Cecil B. DeMille. He explained to me that building up Rousseau as a film personality in his own right would be good for our production. I dropped some big hints about how much I'd like to see Hollywood, but Mr. Varnay insisted that there was plenty for me to do right where I was in New York City.

Mr. Demille *

He told me he wanted me to organize the next four episodes of "Goddess" into shooting scripts, right up to the two climactic episodes which, he said, we would work on together when he returned.

* C. B. DeMille: Celebrity film maker of the teens, '20s, '30s, '40s & '50s.

I was sorry to see my two boys leaving again, but did my best to take it like a trooper.

Mr. Varnay provided me with a stenographer and my own office to work on the script, and I went at it with a will.

And there was war work too. Some evenings Marie and I helped Chick, who was knitting socks for the boys "over there."

I still looked forward to hearing Marie read Lionel's very moving letters from the front. And I was also doing some war work, raising money for war bonds in various places in New York City.

from the trade magazines and through their own grapevine and had heard absolutely nothing about Mr. Varnay and Rousseau in Hollywood! Worse yet, one evening at the Kit kat Club, we saw Cecil B. DeMille in New York.

Lionel's Letters became fewer but even so, I was jealous for, as was the case the year before, I did not receive a letter of any kind from Mr. Varnay.

Another thing that bothered me was this: Allen and Chick kept up on everything that went on in the movie business, both

Allen, at my prompting, introduced me. He was cordial and, while Mr. DeMille seemed familiar with our project and even made polite inquiries about Mr. Varnay, it was rather embarrassingly clear that the two had never met and that Mr. DeMille's next picture, starring Mary Pickford, had no part in it for a dog!

When we got back to our table, Allen tried to assure me that none of this should cause me any concern, but looks he exchanged with Chick when he thought I wasn't looking told another story.

I might have agonized more about it than I did, except right after Christmas something else happened that knocked all of that out of my mind. Marie received a telegram informing her that Lionel had been killed.

Poor Marie was inconsolable! We all were! But I must say, Allen and Chick behaved wonderfully about it. Chick had wanted to enlist for a while, in spite of the strings his father had pulled to keep him out of it. And when Lionel was killed, he felt a renewed urge to join up. Allen had an asthma condition that kept him out, and he urged Chick to reconsider.

The thought of losing little Chick in that horrible war did seem terribly unnecessary and I chimed in with Allen to dissuade him.

After that, though, Chick knitted more socks for the boys than Marie and I combined!

I must say, the reception I gave Mr. Varnay and Rousseau when they returned in the spring was just a bit frosty.

He told me negotiations with DeMille had fallen through. I nodded sarcastically. The fact that he was lying to my face made me livid and I felt sure there must be an affair.

In spite of that, I did my best to get back into work mode on "Goddess" with him. We were nearing the climax now.

But, even as we worked, another menace closer to home appeared: the outbreak of Spanish influenza that was slowly but surely becoming as big a threat to human life as the war.

And when we weren't shooting, I was helping him put together the final two climactic episodes. Though I must say, at this point, he was relying less on my input, which probably wouldn't have ordinarily bothered me so much, if it weren't for his emerging pattern of winter absences that I was now convinced had to be some kind of romantic liaison!

As a result, when he started mapping out the big climax that occurs in the story *after* the seven urns have revealed their vital message to the world, I must say I tended to view the futuristic climax that he was plotting out with something of a jaundiced eye.

In this sequence, set some time in the future, all the dead souls killed in the war begin to be reborn as more highly evolved, advanced beings who grow up rapidly and work together harmoniously to build a better, braver and more enlightened world. When I had the temerity to openly question this, I felt that Mr. Varnay was rather brusque with me. He told me it was just as the talking head had told it to him, although he did admit to "romanticizing it slightly: for public consumption."

When I pressed him on this point, he made a rather odd reply. He said that the war dead *would* be born again, though *not necessarily as human beings!*

That struck me as downright bizarre. But Mr. Varnay nipped my objection in the bud, telling me that the key thing, at this time, was to deliver an optimistic message to the public, showing the potential for a brighter future through better living.

But even as we rushed to finish all the principal photography, the influenza epidemic was about to hit much closer to home. Within mere days of his final scene in the film, Allen Rollins was struck down! It all happened very quickly. He complained of not feeling quite right on the last Friday of our scenes together, and the following Monday he was dead!

I wanted to go to him as soon as I heard he was sick, but Mr. Varnay was worried for my health, as we had been doing kissing scenes. In fact, Mr. Varnay had photographed that final kiss again and again. I remember Allen and I had both laughed when he joked that my kisses were overwhelming him, little realizing it was the early symptoms of his final illness!

In fact, the following day I did feel like I too might have contracted it. And Mr. Varnay sequestered me, treating me with a homeopathic cure of his own creation that I was certain would surely kill me!

However, by Sunday, I was quite recovered and I urged him to try the same cure on poor Allen, but he told me it was too late, that Allen's doctors had informed him that he was already sinking into death. None of this behavior, and what followed, did anything more to endear me to Mr. Varnay.

He would not let me attend Allen's funeral, nor did he seem at all inclined to share his influenza remedy with the world, brusquely referring to the epidemic as a "natural correction," whatever that meant!

Our relationship was definitely showing signs of strain. Not only was there a growing certainty in my mind that he was having an affair, but there was the callous attitude he seemed to have toward humanity at large, even in the midst of his grand utopian schemes! I was beginning to argue openly with him about all of this, throwing all his odd talk about the war dead being reborn as animals right back in his face.

When he countered with a lot of grand talk that various animal species, as they evolved, might be the key to better life for all the beings of the world, I barely heard him. Frankly, I was becoming more and more conviced that I was living with a lunatic, or worse!

When the cold weather set in that year, the influenza epidemic began to spread and my feelings of hostility toward Mr. Varnay, who continued to insist that the epidemic would soon run its course, grew with it.

When he informed me that he and Rousseau were again about to take leave of me, and he didn't even offer much in the way of an excuse this time, I sarcastically observed that perhaps he was planning to enroll Rousseau in a university to further evolve his intellect. But the hurt look on Rousseau's face, showing he clearly understood me, made me regret my remark immediately. Before they left this time, Mr. Varnay was very considerate to me, imploring me to try and have faith in him and in the enterprise we were both involved in.

When he left, we were at something of an uneasy truce, but I still felt both hurt and confused. I just felt that if I were so essential to this so-called enterprise, why was so much about it being withheld from me?

But there was certainly more sorrow around me than my little worries. Marie was still grieving over Lionel, and one thing that had been happening was that our friendship had deepened.

And there was poor Chick. Marie and I had been doing our best to comfort him, as he was taking Allen's death very hard, but with the influenza in full cry, we'd lost track of him. By November all the cabarets and taverns had been closed.

But then by the end of the month, strangely, the influenza epidemic began to lift! Just as everyone began to think it would never end, it began to disappear as mysteriously as it came! It seemed to have run its course just as Mr. Varnay said it would.

The papers were reporting that public places, including all cabarets, would soon be opening their doors again, and Marie heard the Poodle Doodle, Allen and Chick's old club, which never really had an official license, was already open. On the chance that we might find Chick, we decided to go over there.

From the Poodle Doodle's manager, we discovered that the Poodle, being a private club, never actually completely closed and Chick had been living there for the last three and a half weeks! And to judge by the look of him, he hadn't shaved in all that time, changed his clothes, or eaten much. He looked bad. We were appalled by his condition, but did our best to conceal it.

Poor Chick. He'd always been the biggest drinker among us, but now he was going at it with a vengeance, anticipating the kind of drinking that was to become so rampant in the next decade which sadly would claim Chick as one of its earliest casualties.

When a girl singer came on and began to sing, "Keep The Home Fires Burning," a song Chick and Allen had both been quite fond of, Chick snapped.

He stood up and loudly demanded that the girl stop singing...

Then he turned the gun on himself and shouted,

She produced a handkerchief and gently tied it around my wrist, which, in truth, did seem merely grazed. Then she went to speak with the three policemen.

While this went on, I looked at my arm and noticed the initials M.D. stitched on the handkerchief, and I suddenly realized that the woman talking to the police was Muriel Davenport, a well-known figure among New York's well-to-do and notoriously prominent in the city's so called "avant-garde" circles. She had resided in Italy, for the most part, until the outbreak of the war brought her home again.

I looked over again and saw Muriel Davenport hand each of the police officers some money, and she made the musician who had disarmed Chick give them the gun.

said a woman who'd been sitting at Muriel's table earlier and was now sitting next to me. She put a comforting arm around my shoulders.

"Muriel's husband is a dear friend of the Mayor's," she said. It must have been true because now the officers were joking with Muriel, as they pocketed the cash she had given them, along with the pistol, and had left, making no attempt to arrest Chick. He was now slumped at a table, with his head buried in his arms, while Marie did her best to comfort him.

Now that the police were gone, Muriel turned back to our table. She raised an eyebrow when she noticed her companion still with her arm around me, but then smiled broadly as she glided over and introduced herself. Then looking at her companion, she somewhat frostily said,

It was hard to tell whether it was a question or an accusation, but it was gradually dawning on me that

Muriel and her companion were apparently more than just friends. Of course, that shouldn't have seemed surprising to me since the Poodle Doodle largely catered to people who were outside the norm, especially in things sexual.

When I introduced Marie to Muriel and her companion, who was a fairly well-known poet who went only by the name of Holda, it seemed fairly clear that they thought we were "romantically" involved.

But, on the other hand, they seemed completely willing to accept Marie socially, so we were willing enough to let them think what they wanted about the other.

The fact is we were both rather charmed by Muriel. On the other hand, it took us both a while to become accustomed to Holda's rather "forward" manner. Muriel told us we should just ignore Holda's "little peculiarities."

So began my bohemian phase. I'd experienced it superficially with Allen and Chick at the Poodle and several other haunts they took us to, but Muriel now put us on the "inside track" of that world, so to speak.

Quite frankly, I would have been less open to this earlier, but I had acquired a certain notoriety from all the "Goddess" publicity. Over time, it had become something of a social impediment in the city's higher circles. Mr. Varnay assured me that this would change when the film and its message caught on.

But, at this time, the snide remark the indecent proposal and the cold shoulder were becoming increasingly frequent occurrences. Consequently, Muriel's warm acceptance of both Marie and myself was a refreshing change for both of us.

At the Provincetown Playhouse, I met Eugene O'Neill.

At a party afterwards,

George Cram Cook, who managed the playhouse, asked if I'd be interested in appearing in a play he was writing. I was flattered, but didn't think it was something Mr. Varnay would approve of. I still felt I owed him something in spite of our strained relationship.

However, Marie's expert dancing had been attracting attention, and not long after that, Holda made Marie an offer to appear in a dancing role in a play she told Marie she had written especially for her. Neither Marie nor I really understood Holda's play, but there was something wonderfully striking about it. And it did excellent business for about a week,

...until the Police closed it down.

Chapter Ten: War's Aftermath

This was a sign of the coming times, as we would soon fully find out when Mr. Varnay and Rousseau returned in the spring of 1919.

I was worried about what he would think of my bohemian phase, and it might have been more of a problem if it weren't for the big fuss Muriel Davenport made over him when I introduced them. She immediately invited him to be the guest of honor at one of her evenings. I think there was something about Muriel's eagerness to accept him exactly as he was that attracted him to her in the same way she had attracted Marie and myself. It certainly seemed that way when he showed up one evening in full 18th-century regalia, creating quite a splash.

Muriel's crowd, for the most part, listened to everything he had to say with good grace, though I couldn't help noticing a certain patronizing condescension among some there at the utopian sunniness of his presentation.

Such as it was, it had to go a long way, for 1919 was certainly showing signs of certain reactionary post-war social trends. By the time Mr. Varnay had edited "The Goddess of Enlightenment" and was ready to release it, he immediately ran afoul of the censors! What had been deemed acceptable in terms of nudity a few years earlier was no longer the case. Trashier films of the kind had caused a crackdown. But this was merely where the trouble began.

A nudie exploitation film from 1919.

His budding association with the avant-garde movement was looked on with suspicion in certain powerful circles and within that context, his "enlightened" Christianity was also warily regarded. It was even suggested that, as it had no official church sanction, there must be something heretical about it, even communistic.

And that was something that was causing problems for a lot of people just then. There were growing signs in the air of what was being called a red scare. Young J. Edgar Hoover, not yet fully in charge of the FBI, was nonetheless organizing mass deportations of

any aliens at all suspected of anything remotely smacking of sedition. This gave Mr. Varnay, a native of France, good cause for worry!

When it became increasingly clear that Mr. Varnay was not going to get "Goddess" distributed, he decided to take another approach, with Muriel Davenport's help. She agreed to hold another soirée for Mr. Varnay, inviting all the most influential people she knew, where he could give a lecture and preview portions of the film. Well, not only was it poorly attended, but as soon as the film began running, the police raided, seized the print and arrested Mr. Varnay and myself.

Final

DAILY NEWS

2¢

DOG BITES COP IN SOCIETY RAID

Savage Beast To Be Destroyed

"Naked" Girl Defies Police! page 2

The just launched Daily News throws in their two cents.

The press had a field day. And while we were being held without bail for the next few days, Rousseau came within a hair's breadth of being destroyed!

We could only thank providence that Muriel finally came to our rescue, getting a stay for Rousseau at the very last minute and bail, finally, for Mr. Varnay and myself.

Worse yet, during the raid,

...Rousseau bit a police officer and was also taken into custody!

Once he was out, Mr. Varnay immediately began plans to take his case directly to the public. He rented Webster Hall, where he planned to show all fifteen episodes of "The Goddess of Enlightenment," free of charge to the public. To say that this quixotic move worried me is putting it mildly! He seemed to have forgotten poor Rousseau, still in custody, entirely! Again, Muriel came to our rescue. Apparently she succeeded to some extent, in private, with the powers that be in New York City, where she'd failed before, publicly.

She informed us that she was about to sail to Europe to re-open her Italian villa that had been closed for the last three years of the war. The state of New York was unofficially offering to release Rousseau if Mr. Varnay would drop his plans for a public show of "The Goddess of Enlightenment" and voluntarily leave with Muriel for Europe. Otherwise, it was strongly implied that deportation proceedings for him would go forward and Rousseau would be immediately destroyed.

As far as I was concerned, the safety of Rousseau was reason enough for immediate acceptance, and watching him strut up and down for a full fifteen minutes before deciding annoyed me almost beyond endurance!

However, in the end, in the late spring of 1919, Mr. Varnay, Rousseau, Marie, and I set sail for Italy with Muriel and her entourage. He even managed to get the massive negative of "Goddess" on board with us. It was my first

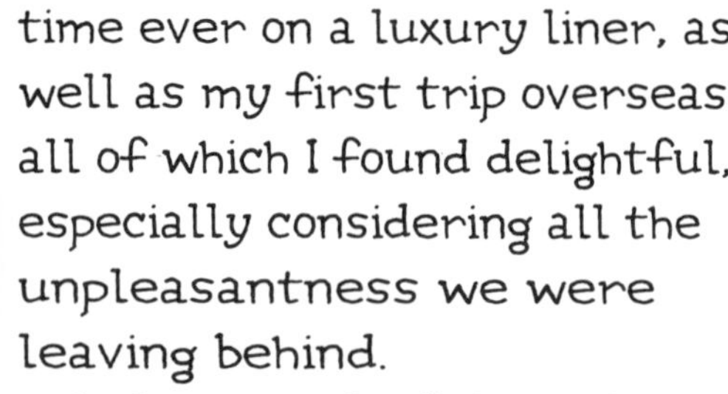

time ever on a luxury liner, as well as my first trip overseas, all of which I found delightful, especially considering all the unpleasantness we were leaving behind.

Italy, a wonderful revelation to me and Florence, where Muriel's villa was located, showed little sign of the long, bloody war that just ended. At first we were Muriel's guests at her enormous villa, but it was fast filling

up with her various bohemian friends to the point that it was almost like a small expatriate village unto itself.

One small snag in the arrangement was that the Count, who seemed rather sweet on Marie, insisted that he be allowed to occupy one room of the villa as part of the arrangement. This might have been more of a problem than it sounds like, if it weren't for the fact that Marie seemed to return the Count's affections. Indeed, the Count, a fine musician, proved to be good company and in no way seemed to show any sign of interfering

with either Mr. Varnay's privacy, or his ongoing plans.

What those plans immediately consisted of were that he set up a private theater in the villa and began to put on showings of "The Goddess of Enlightenment" for anyone who was interested, hoping, of course, to sooner or later attract a European distributor. All through that summer he showed the film. Curiously, I found myself back in my old job, after a fashion, playing for the movies. But this time I had Rousseau by my side, contributing his unique harmony. In fact, at the climax, Mr. Varnay joined in, adding more harmony as I sang a song that Mr. Varnay had written, called "My Lady of Enlightenment." The effect was quite exhilarating, at least to us.

Unfortunately, the film's optimistic message, as well as its preachy climax, wasn't really what war-weary Europeans were looking to divert themselves with. In any event, no distribution deal materialized.

This may have had something to do with Mr. Varnay's surprising enthusiasm for the project. He decided that Marie's wedding, which he insisted on hosting, would be *the* big social event at the end of the summer season.

At her wedding, which he appeared at in the most outrageously dandified 18th-century costume I'd ever seen him in, he personally gave the bride away. What is more, I happen to know he bestowed a rather generous dowry on Severino. It was a thing he didn't really have to do, and I found it touching.

Note: Marie's Futurist dress, her attendants' costumes and the Count's wedding suit were designed by Severino himself.

Of course, it made Mr. Varnay and Rousseau's inevitable departure later that Fall all the more upsetting. No longer did I have the consolation of Marie's company.

His excuse this time was that he wanted to investigate purchasing a farm or vineyard to set up a commune of sorts to give a fresh start to some of the displaced refugees of the European war.

It seemed particularly thin to me, and when I pointed out to him that the land on the Count's former estate might work perfectly well for such a plan, he merely kissed me on the cheek and again urged me to try and have some faith in him.

He left a couple of foppy tutors, but I was determined to have nothing to do with them. This didn't seem to bother them in the least, as they seemed far more interested in each other than they were in me.

For all the wonderful gaiety that the villa had all summer, suddenly it seemed very lonely indeed. Even Muriel Davenport had suddenly decided to tour the new Soviet Union. Quite honestly, I don't know what I would have done at that point, when an unexpected letter set me on quite another path.

Out of nowhere, I got a letter from Lumberton, from my brother, Andrew! From the postmarks, I could see it had traveled quite a few places in its search for me. Apparently, Lumberton had fallen on hard times. The lumber up river had all played out, causing quite an exodus from the area.

Andrew was getting by, raising corn for the Brauntons' distillery, now being run by Wolf Braunton. Since the death of Wolf's father, even that business wasn't going well. And with the coming of Prohibition, it stood a chance of being shut down altogether.

Basically, Andrew was asking for a loan to tide him and his new family over for the winter.

I knew I could scrape something together to send him, but then it occurred to me that perhaps I could do better than that. Perhaps this was a sign for me to finally tear away from the frustrating life I had been living these last few years. And so I left Italy, leaving not even a forwarding address.

Chapter Eleven: Return to Lumberton
Two weeks later, I arrived at Lumberton's wooden pier at just about 9A.M.
I had to pay the boat extra to let me off there as Lumberton was no longer one of its regular stops,
and when I got off, I saw why: there wasn't a soul to be seen along Lumberton's only rickety street of commerce; not that it teemed with people in its best days, but you could always count on seeing a few loafers hanging about.
And something else:
when I lived there, buzzing saws of the two mills almost never stopped during the day. Now it was eerily quiet except for the cawing of a few crows and the splashing noise of the river behind me. Without thinking, I wandered over to the Isis.
A decaying Tom Mix poster from about two years ago gave me a fair idea of about how long it had been closed.
HOTEL
LOADING
VENTURE
TODAY
TOM MIX

Well, closed wasn't exactly right. The door was open and I heard the hurried scurrying of animals as I wandered in, and plenty

of evidence of critters at my feet, too.

But the thing that startled me most was that, in its abandoned lobby, they'd set up that plaster copy of the nude statue that looked like me!

It was chipped in places and there was rude writing on it. It made me mad! I spit on my handkerchief and was trying to rub a rude saying off

when I suddenly heard an all too familiar voice say,

So ya know yourself, do ya?

It was Wolf Braunton, although if I hadn't instantly recognized his insolent rasping voice, I'm not sure I would have recognized him right off. But he was the same old animal on two legs without feathers, even if the legs didn't seem any too steady.

When I told him I was there to help my brother, Andrew, he laughed heartily,

which quickly turned into a series of coughs that made me turn and cover my face.

After recovering himself he told me with open mockery that Andrew was going to need plenty of help. He told me the corn crop Andrew had just harvested was scarcely worth the effort and the rent on the shack that he and his family lived in was three months overdue,

...and if he doesn't kick in soon, I'm throwing those dead-beats out!

Then he stopped and seemed to be taking a good long look at me.

I've got to say, Kate, the last few years ain't exactly done bad by you.

I could kinda forget the rent, maybe even put the bunch of 'em in the hotel across the street.

Not the best room, of course; that's where you and me,

That is just about as far as I let him go on that one, and if it wasn't for the fact that I came to help Andrew and his family, I would have arranged to get out of Lumberton as soon as possible. Instead I had him give me a reckoning of what rent Andrew owed, paid the creature, and walked out.

Most of the shacks where Lumberton mill hands used to live had been torn down to make room for land to grow corn on, and I could see evidence of the recently harvested crop.

I saw three shacks standing and started toward them. As I got closer, I could hear the cries of children and

a shrill woman's voice, which made it pretty easy to know which shack Andrew's family was in.

I knocked several times and when no one answered the door, I walked in.

I recognized the woman as Maud Banks. I'd taught her in school and remembered her as a not particularly apt student. I will say, though, my sudden appearance certainly did shut her up, if not her offspring.
NOVEMBER
A little boy, who appeared to be about two, was running around in circles, screaming at the top of his lungs. Maud was trying to nurse an infant that I later learned was a girl, but from her wails, I wondered if Maud really had any milk to give her.
There were suspicious marks on Maud's face that made one suspect violence on Andrew's part. And there was certainly no love in Maud's voice when she told me I'd find Andrew in back. A blanket had been hung to suggest a second room. Maud turned her head in that direction and yelled, but there was no response.
He only passed out at daybreak. I wouldn't wake him if I was *you*.
In spite of Maud's warning, I walked behind the blanket and there was Andrew snoring, fully dressed in clothes so matted I doubt if he'd had them completely off in weeks. He was sprawled on an old bed frame stuffed with straw, covered with a matted old sheet!
One hand was still reaching for an empty bottle. He was one sorry-looking mess and just then,
it shames me to say it, but, frankly, I was sorry I came.

Chapter Twelve: Some Surprises

Well, I did what I could for the next few months, starting with getting Andrew sobered up. Over the winter I'd ordered a bunch of government farm bulletins, taking in some basic information about crop rotation and soil fertilization, and by the following March, I was ready to supervise putting in a new corn crop.

Of course, it stuck in my craw to be contributing to Wolf Braunton's now clearly illegal corn distillery, but just then it seemed to be the only game in town. Although, I *was* also experimenting with a tomato crop and a few other things I had been reading up on.

It was one of the first sunny days in March in 1921, and Andrew and I were planting corn seed in a field that Andrew had plowed just the day before. I'd reached into the sack to sprinkle some corn into another plowed furrow of soil when I heard a very distinctive barking that I knew very well indeed. I stood and turned and running for me was Rousseau!

In mere seconds, he was pawing at me! I was so ecstatically happy to see him that I grabbed him up in my arms! (No small handful either!) Soon he was maniacally licking my face and whining with joy.

After a mutually joyful moment, I set him down. I kneeled while still talking to him as he squealed back.

Then, for the first time, I thought, how? And looking beyond Rousseau, many yards beyond him, I noticed a lone figure, hat in hand. The sun behind him showed him in stark silhouette but, of course, I knew it was Mr. Varnay.

Not only was I shocked to see him, but I was surprised at how very glad I was to see both of them. I ran over, with Rousseau hot on my heels,

and kissed him.

He seemed extremely glad to see me. Though in a suit, there was nothing at all ostentatious about his dress or manner. In fact, I'd never seen him looking so humble before.

He told me he'd found the envelope from Andrew's letter and he took a chance that he'd find me here in Lumberton. And he told me he'd been devastated to find me gone from the villa when he and Rousseau had returned.

Since formal deportation proceedings had never been started against him, he had little trouble getting back into the country. And should anything come up, he'd been led to understand that the new administration in Washington could be "reasoned" with. Money talked loud and clear now, and Mr. Varnay still had some.

As he continued talking, I noticed that his old cocksure manner was coming back. He told me I could forget about putting in a big corn crop for Wolf Braunton's distillery, as he'd just bought Lumberton lock, stock and barrel from Braunton.

His eyes positively gleamed as he next loftily informed me that he intended to establish an experimental communal farm for the distressed people in the area who were in need of food, shelter and employment. As he raved on in this view, with growing bluster, my initial joy at seeing him was beginning to diminish.

Finally I broke in on this bombastically tiresome soliloquy and said, "What a lot of rot!"

He readily conceded that he knew nothing about it, but quickly added that this was where we could succeed together. He picked up an open farm bulletin that I'd been studying. He told me he'd never said it before, but he was saying it now.

And besides all that, *I* need *you*!

I know *you* feel a lot of frustration but *I love you* and I pledge to do everything I can to change things for the better for *all* of the world but especially for *you*, Kate!

I was touched, if not altogether convinced, and felt further obliged to air my grievances. Not just all the frustrations of our relationship, but especially those mysterious disappearances! I told him that if he was having an affair, why not just come out with it and tell me! It would be kinder than all this deception.

At this point, he told me he simply wasn't in a position to explain his annual absences to me but swore quite fervently that no love affairs had any part of it. He finished by pledging that one day I would know it all. I wasn't really satisfied by all this, but somehow I believed that he was sincere.

And so, in the coming months, I went at learning farming with a will. Several of Andrew's other unemployed logger friends showed up. None of them knew any more about raising crops than I did, but I was learning and by

early summer we had a better looking corn crop than I'd dared hope for. I also had some coops put in and bought some chickens.

Other than supplying money, Mr. Varnay didn't really participate. He'd taken over the top floor of the hotel as his headquarters. He *did*, however, bring in some workers to erect an imposing dome-like building of concrete and offered no explanation whatsoever as to what it was to be used for. When it was completed, he had it locked up and kept the only key for himself.

Karl Braunton, who was in sorrier shape than Wolf, continued to occupy the old Braunton tavern, even though it no longer belonged to him. Mr. Varnay seemed willing enough to let him squat there for the time being, as Karl seemed willing enough to stay out of everyone's way. So much so that when he died, no one was immediately aware of it until a stench that grew gradually made it obvious!

Karl's death aside, things gradually began to settle into a fairly good routine and soon most of our crop was ready for harvesting. There had been some unexpected problems. The biggest one was that the insects had taken their toll on what I thought was going to be a promising tomato crop. Even the corn, which had looked so promising and was larger than Andrew's last crop, or so he told me, was still disappointing. Mr. Varnay took an active role in storing it all in our very modern-looking corn crib. I'd ordered it prefabricated and had it set up a few months earlier.

Soon Mr. Varnay and Rousseau were again getting ready to take their annual leave of us, and he left me with more than enough money to keep things going through the winter. Sensing that my frustrations ran deeper than just his leave taking, he did his best to be encouraging.

He told me that all things considered, I had done remarkably well, and he suggested that I look into finding an experienced farmer who could function as something of a foreman, someone who knew the business of farming and could show me how to set things up on a more efficient basis. He told me he felt this was the one thing missing in our current set-up and felt strongly that such a move could radically improve things. The conviction in his manner as he said this was a thing that stayed with me. But before I could do anything about hiring anyone, something quite surprising occurred!

One morning, while I was waiting for the morning ferry with one of my men to bring in some supplies, another boat sailed by. And, as it made no attempt to stop, I saw several burly-looking crewmen pitch three men overboard! They were about thirty yards out and I immediately got the man with me to row out to where these men were floundering and loudly yelling for help.

A few moments later, we were pulling in three of the sorriest-looking specimens of humanity I ever laid eyes on. Even their unexpected bath in the Chemung River hadn't done much to get rid of their collective and fearfully pungent smell. While they were sputtering thanks, I looked them dubiously over, and gradually it hit me.

Chick?

There was Chick, looking far worse than the time we found him living at the Poodle Doodle!

Kate!

His friends, if that is indeed what they were, were quite another matter. If it weren't for the fact that they were Chick's companions, I would have found some way to get rid of them. As it was, I stretched a point, which is something I would have cause to regret.

Once on shore, Chick told me he'd heard about the communal farm I'd established,

and he and his "friends" had come to offer their services. I soon learned from Chick, who I really was glad to see, in spite of the bad company that had attached itself to him, that his father had died. He'd left a rather substantial fortune to Chick, who'd managed to squander it away in something like record time.

Chapter Thirteen: Mr. Wright

It was a bad situation, and it made me all the more eager to find someone to manage the farm as Mr. Varnay had advised. I'd placed ads in several farm journals and was surprised to get a good response sooner than I'd expected and was much closer to home, too – on the other side, more or less, of the Chemung River!

About three weeks after placing the ads, a man named Frank Wright, who had a large farm a few miles inland on the other side of the river, motor-boated over to see me.

Well! I'd be lying if I said I wasn't impressed by this man's personal magnetism. I soon learned that he was college educated, although there was nothing about him that suggested conceit. He quietly took notes as I showed him around, and I could feel myself being drawn to him.

When I'd finished, rather than go into a long spiel, Frank Wright motored me across the river in his boat and drove me a few miles inland to his farm. I'm afraid the stark contrast between my efforts and Frank's modern, scientific operation was quite devastating. For all of that, Frank was quick to praise my fledgling efforts and offered his help.

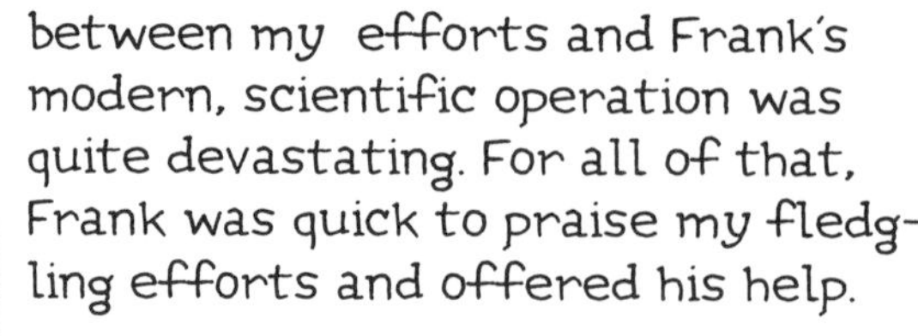

He told me things were humming along well enough on his farm, but that he was eager to experiment with raising soybeans, a crop that he felt would do well in my soil.

Surprisingly, Frank offered to overhaul my operation, without salary, for a percentage of the crop.

He also told me some of his thoughts about farming soybeans. While he wasn't a total vegetarian, he had some rather advanced ideas about soybeans, feeling that they had the potential to replace much and perhaps, in time, all the animal meat in the human diet, which he felt would be much better in many ways.

For one thing, more people in the world could be fed on grain now being used to feed animals raised for meat.

THE MARCH OF HUMANITY
in six stages

I was fascinated and was feeling more and more certain about the entire situation. After all, hiring someone like Frank Wright *was* Mr. Varnay's own idea.

Not only that, Mr. Varnay had predicted that good things would come of it.

I began to feel strongly that this man really was the key missing piece in all of Mr. Varnay's plans for me. Why, he even looked uncannily like the drawing of the more highly evolved males to come in Mr. Varnay's human evolution charts!

And I soon also discovered that he was a natural leader of men.

He'd duly noticed the drunkenness of Chick and his companions on his initial tour of the farm. Once he'd taken charge of things, he'd discovered a substantial deficiency in our corn crib. It turned out that some of the corn was being secretly used to distill liquor in part of our closed-down distillery.

Chick's two companions had not been totally idle.

Besides drinking the stuff, they'd begun to sell the booze they'd been making to the other men on the farm! Frank lost no time in running Chick's two pals off the farm, and it was only my direct intervention that saved Chick from being included.

Frank then called a meeting with Andrew and my other hands and laid down the law. He told them liquor would no longer be tolerated and they could henceforth do things his way or they could get out. They all stayed, including Chick.

I'd like to say that all went smoothly from that point on. To a great extent it did, but with one horribly sad exception. About two weeks later, Chick was found dead. He'd gotten some cleaning fluid with a lot of alcohol in it and drunk it. Poor little Chick. I was very devastated over this!

Frank had him buried on the property and even spoke touchingly over his grave.

It was the one sour note that Fall and Winter.

The really big news, from my perspective, was that Frank and I slowly but surely had become lovers. You know, Ellie, I was hesitant to mention this matter to you in spite of the fact that sex before marriage has become so common in today's world. But in all honesty, I think the one real difference between then and now comes down to one single word: discretion.

People are more open about discussing these things today, perhaps too much so. I will not belabor the point, except to say, I mention this to you solely in the interest of being better understood.

You must understand, Ellie, this was a really big thing to me. It was a great missing thing in my life, and brought me a real feeling of joy and fulfillment. And I felt quite certain that this union would get Mr. Varnay's enthusiastic endorsement. It just seemed to fit so well with everything he'd always said, including his most recent prediction about the success I would have with a new foreman.

Chapter Fourteen: Disappointments

Well, the outcome of this situation was disappointing. Upon his return, Mr. Varnay initially seemed impressed with all of Frank's innovations, even his theories about substituting soy products for animal meat. I was thrilled by this initial good impression and so was all the more shocked at how badly he took the news that something romantic had developed between Frank and myself.

At first he seemed calm enough as he went through a long, obtuse and increasingly irrational list of objections and reasons why Frank was wrong as a mate for me. But when he saw that these arguments were not reaching me, things became more hostile.

I was so knocked off balance by this that I dared not bring up the fact that our relationship had already been consummated. But within myself, I had already decided to leave Mr. Varnay and marry Frank Wright.

However, I was even more surprised by Frank's reaction. He seemed disturbed, but counseled patience. He suggested that we should suspend our relationship for the time being, feeling that he could win Varnay over in time. And so, for a while, Frank continued to work the farm. But, predictably enough, the relationship between him and Mr. Varnay began to sour.

It wasn't long after that that Frank came and told me that he was leaving. Worse yet, he told me, gently enough I suppose, that he was starting to feel that perhaps our relationship had been a mistake. He threw in, I guess as a sort of consolation, that he was willing to buy all the soybeans we were willing to sell him.

To say I was devastated hardly does justice to the way this made me feel! I think that the main reason that I didn't just up and leave the farm was the good effect Frank's leadership had on Andrew and his family and the other loggers who had followed Andrew to the farm. Of course, even though Frank was leaving, he promised his continued help in an unofficial capacity.

I guess part of me was clinging to the idea that things between Frank and me might still eventually work out. Of course, his unwillingness to fight for me seemed to be a pretty clear sign that Frank Wright was probably wrong for me.

So things muddled along. Even with Frank more out of the picture, Mr. Varnay seemed in no way elated at the turn of events and he was spending more time by himself.
When he wasn't off in his domed concrete headquarters, he could usually be seen out by a brook that flowed out of the Chemung river out onto our property....
...where some beavers had constructed a rather ambitious dam.

When Varnay and Rousseau again took their leave late that fall, general morale on the farm was not good. Not very long after, Andrew came to me and told me he was quitting and going across the river to work for Frank. He told me things had just gotten too strange on the farm to suit him.

My God! I'd gone to a considerable amount of trouble for Andrew, and I'm afraid I let him have it. The idea of his leaving me flat after all that staggered me!

Well, at least he had the good grace to look ashamed. After I rather heatedly pointed all this out to him, he expressed gratitude to me. But as I looked at him as he spoke, something very significant struck me. Whatever I had started in terms of rehabilitating Andrew, Frank Wright had completed.

In spite of my disappointment, and I was disappointed, the look in his eye, the clear sense of purpose that showed in his manner was very impressive. And I could think of little else to say to him finally, other than to wish him luck.

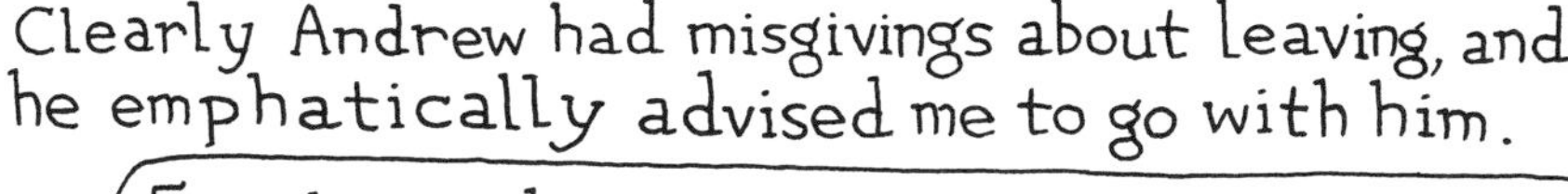

Clearly Andrew had misgivings about leaving, and he emphatically advised me to go with him.

"Frank Wright is crazy about you and would marry you in a minute," he told me. "Why don't you show some gumption and go to him instead of wasting any more time on that crackpot, Varnay!"

I was very much conflicted and more than half believed that Andrew was right. But when I half-heartedly tried to defend Mr. Varnay, he took a parting shot.

He told me that if Mr. Varnay was so much on the up and up, what was going on in that mysterious, domed cement building that Mr. Varnay wouldn't let anyone go near? Andrew clearly implied that something illegal must be going on. I didn't really think it was true, but after Andrew left, I decided to see for myself.

Chapter 15: A Big Surprise
A lot of thoughts about all that had happened were swirling through my mind by this time. I was certain that, in his own strange way, Mr. Varnay really did love me. But there was so much about himself that he seemed so unwilling to share with me! I didn't like the idea of violating his privacy, but if there were something wrong, something really wrong going on, I was determined, now more than ever, to find it out. A large set of wire cutters broke the lock on the door easily enough.
I guess the biggest initial surprise was that there was very little stored there, other than a pair of wooden boxes connect-ed to a vat of fluid.
But it was what I found in those boxes that gave me the shock of my life!
Inside the two boxes were Mr. Varnay and Rousseau.
At first, I thought they were dead, but when I screamed, I saw Mr. Varnay stir slightly. When he finally recognized me,

he seemed utterly horrified.
Pulling himself into a sitting position, he shakily demanded that I hand him a jar of liquid on a nearby counter.
After drinking some of it,
he got out of the box, still very unsteady, and went to the smaller box that contained Rousseau, who seemed rather ominously stiff.
There's no time to lose!
he gasped. And, after making me lock the cement building, he had me assist him in heating and mixing several chemical compounds.

When he was done, he drew the liquid into a syringe and injected it into a vein in Rousseau's neck. He was devastated when it seemed to have no noticeable effect on the poor creature. This just about broke my heart. That I might have killed Rousseau by my snooping was unbearable to me! Varnay, still shaky, urged me to brace up.

We may still be able to save him, he said,

We warmed Rousseau's body, which was beginning to ominously chill, in a tub of water that I constantly replaced with more water that I was continuously heating on the kitchen stove.

Finally, when Varnay was satisfied that his body was supple enough, he again injected the chemicals into Rousseau's neck.

A few moments later, to my unutterable joy, I heard a faint doggy whimper. Then in the midst of this unbelievably strange scene, Rousseau slowly opened his eyes.

Finally, after an unnaturally long pause, he looked at me again and said, I guess there's a lot to explain.

Well, that was true, and I waited silently. Speaking rather low and haltingly, for he was still far from recovered, he began to explain to me that everything that I had just witnessed was really far less strange than it actually seemed.

He told me that just as other mammals had the ability to hibernate, he had discovered a way of doing something similar.

It's not black magic,

he said,

but merely an application of natural science utilizing certain easily obtained herbs that ultimately have the potential to extend human life.

He told me that while it seemed to work in a satisfactory manner, he was not yet ready to share this discovery.

I still need to evaluate certain side effects that the procedure might possibly have over time.

He said that he and Rousseau were older than they appeared to be, but when I asked him *how* much older, he seemed not to hear me. In fact, I never did find out how old Mr. Varnay really was.

Weird as all this was, it actually did ease much of the tension that had grown between us in the five years I had known him. It made me feel more sympathetic as I now felt fairly sure that sexuality and to some extent his diminished feelings toward me may have been unfortunate side effects of his discovery.

Unfortunately, the rest of the farmhands soon followed Andrew's example and left to work for Frank Wright. A short time later, Frank came and offered to let two of his men continue to help with the soy crop. I'm afraid I rather coldly refused. I could see a definite sadness in his face, and I felt pretty sure that he too felt pain at our parting. It struck me that Andrew was probably right. If I actually took the initiative to leave Mr. Varnay, I think Frank and I might have had a future together. But knowing what I then knew, I felt I couldn't leave Mr. Varnay.

Mr. Varnay and Rousseau did not go back into their hibernation state that year, but neither looked very well. And I sensed a growing sadness that seemed to be taking him over. When I would try to make conversation, he'd simply say,

Outside of the soybeans Frank continued to buy from me, it was mainly vegetables for our own immediate needs.

By the late fall of 1922, when Mr. Varnay and Rousseau prepared to go into hibernation, I felt a real panic at the idea of being left all alone, and my request to hibernate with them seemed to please him.

And so, having established myself in this strange routine, the years rolled on, not that you could tell from looking at me.

But it also left me feeling quite queer inside, not at all really in the proper flow of nature.

I still continued to see Frank Wright several times a year, when he'd come over on soybean business. Over time, he became rather complimentary about how youthful looking I still was, and it was true, too.

The other day, Ellie, when I was looking in an old drawer for my spare reading glasses, I found an old photo Andrew took in 1941, and I swear I don't look a day older than the day I first met Frank Wright!

Of course Frank had aged, but gracefully. He's in the picture too, along with his wife and two children.

I suppose that fact should have made me more regretful

than it does, but Frank looks so happy, probably more happy than he ever would have been with me.

As for myself, I felt well enough physically but, well, just generally less emotional. Maybe that wasn't so great but, I don't know. It *was* a substitute of sorts for the pain and loneliness I might otherwise have been feeling by then.

Of course, it did make me better understand Mr. Varnay's growing remoteness. More and more he was spending his time studying the habits of the beavers that lived on a stream on our property. Well, by this time, it was considerably more than a stream. Gradually they

had taken over more and more of our unused farmland. Their one dam had multiplied by now and their various streams and lodges now covered several acres of our land.

I guess I would have to say, at this point, I was really closer friends with Rousseau than I was with Mr. Varnay. But even Rousseau seemed more distant than in earlier years! And deep inside, I couldn't shake a twinge of guilt I felt that some of it may have been my fault for the time I'd abruptly broken in on their long winter's sleep. Neither had seemed quite the same after that.

The coming of World War Two seemed to throw Mr. Varnay even further into himself. When we did talk, the growing theme seemed to be one of regret – that his life's work had been a failure.

On the other hand, it was at about this time that Frank again became a bigger part of my life. He encouraged me to expand my garden for the war effort. So for about three years, I again saw Frank every day except, of course, for my winter absences.

This was scarcely noticed by Mr. Varnay. About the only time he and Frank came close to clashing was when Frank wanted to reclaim some of the land the beavers had taken over.

I could tell Frank found this rather odd. And then there was the fact that I was nearing fifty and still looked half that age. I think what bothered me most about Frank was that the looks of regret that he sometimes cast in my direction were beginning to seem more like looks of pity.

Frank had disappointed me. Perhaps he wasn't quite as perfect as I first thought him to be; but then, who was?

When he finally died, about ten years ago, I went to his funeral, which must have been the first time in many years that I had left my property. I saw his wife and his two children there too. Well, not children now, but middle-aged adults with fine-looking broods of children of their own. I found it strangely comforting.

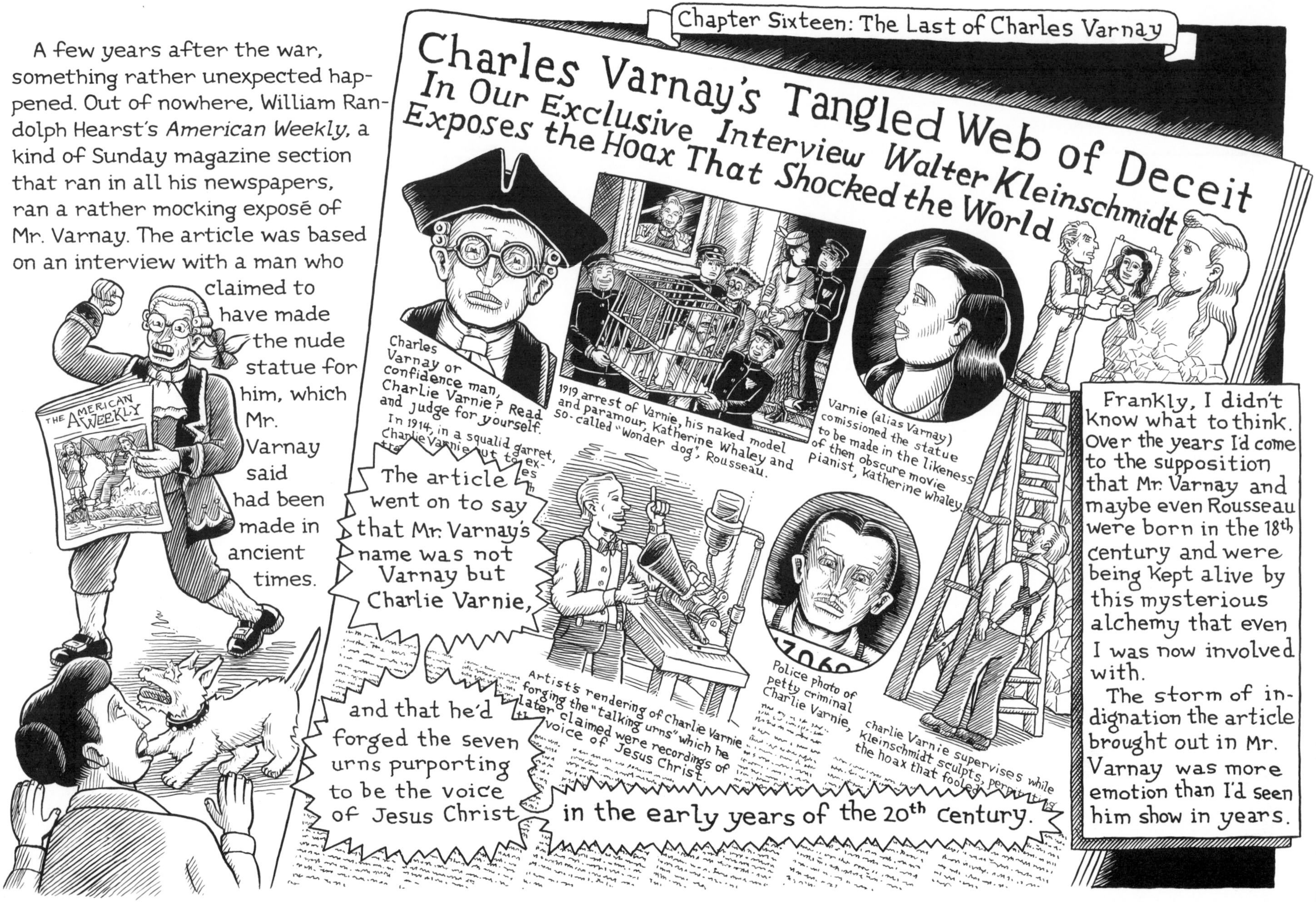

A few years after the war, something rather unexpected happened. Out of nowhere, William Randolph Hearst's *American Weekly*, a kind of Sunday magazine section that ran in all his newspapers, ran a rather mocking exposé of Mr. Varnay. The article was based on an interview with a man who claimed to have made the nude statue for him, which Mr. Varnay said had been made in ancient times.

THE AMERICAN WEEKLY

Chapter Sixteen: The Last of Charles Varnay

Charles Varnay's Tangled Web of Deceit

In Our Exclusive Interview Walter Kleinschmidt Exposes the Hoax That Shocked the World

Charles Varnay or confidence man, Charlie Varnie? Read and judge for yourself.

In 1914, in a squalid garret, Charlie Varnie

1919 arrest of Varnie, his naked model and paramour, Katherine Whaley and so-called "Wonder dog", Rousseau.

Varnie (alias Varnay) comissioned the statue to be made in the likeness of then obscure movie pianist, Katherine Whaley.

The article went on to say that Mr. Varnay's name was not Varnay but Charlie Varnie,

Artist's rendering of Charlie Varnie forging the "talking urns" which he later claimed were recordings of voice of Jesus Christ.

Police photo of petty criminal Charlie Varnie,

Charlie Varnie supervises while Kleinschmidt sculpts, perpetrating the hoax that fooled

and that he'd forged the seven urns purporting to be the voice of Jesus Christ

in the early years of the 20th century.

Frankly, I didn't know what to think. Over the years I'd come to the supposition that Mr. Varnay and maybe even Rousseau were born in the 18th century and were being kept alive by this mysterious alchemy that even I was now involved with.

The storm of indignation the article brought out in Mr. Varnay was more emotion than I'd seen him show in years.

But he also seemed rather embarrassed! I think it was the doubt he sensed that it raised in my mind that bothered him the most!

In the end he decided to go and confront his accuser. As he prepared to leave, I was surprised to learn that he was not planning to take Rousseau! When I asked him about this, he told me I should regard it as a sign that he would return very soon, vindicated. The next day he kissed me, more fervently than he ever had before, and departed.

Charles Varnay's Tangled Web of Deceit
In Our Exclusive Interview Walter Kleinschmidt Exposes the Hoax That Shocked the World

About a month later, I received a letter from him, postmarked from San Fransico. In it, he told me the man who gave the *American Weekly* interview could not be found. He went on to say the doubts of the world mattered little to him, but *my* doubts, which he correctly observed in me, wounded him deeply. Thus he felt compelled to track down this man and make him recant. I never saw or heard from Mr. Varnay again.

One big decision I made at this time was to stop going into those strange hibernations, but, as soon as winter began to set in, Rousseau began to whiningly expect me to prepare him for hibernation. And I dutifully prepared things for him, the herbs and everything else involved, which Mr. Varnay had carefully taught me.

I did this for thirteen more years until, in the spring of 1960, he simply did not wake up. Still, by my reckoning, I had known Rousseau for forty-four years.

About fifteen years ago, I noticed the beaver activity now extended all the way to Mr. Varnay's old cement hide-away, which they seemed to have incorporated into an increasingly complex network of dams and lodges.
HOTEL
Rather than stand in their way, I moved to the abandoned hotel on Lumberton's main street, where I have been living ever since.

Chapter Seventeen: Conclusion
Well, Ellie, there you have it. Mine has certainly been an unusual life. Whether it's been a success or a failure, I really can't say. It *has* been interesting, very odd, often quite lonely and, yes, rather frustrating.
To be so close to understanding the mysteries of life and then not to achieve that understanding is, of course, *very* frustrating; then again, it's not so unique. Many people *think* they understand what life is all about; theories abound and conflict. Wars are fought over it and yet no consensus ever seems to emerge.
At the same time, scientific achievement soars on in the midst of human chaos and conflict. So, we've also reached the point of showing that
the human race may be on the verge of self extinction, even as scientific achievement seems to move forward. It's a puzzle, Ellie, and one that I am frankly incapable of solving.

Epilogue

This is where Kate's manuscript ends. Whether it was interrupted by her death is not certain, but the story does have a postscript. In the letter that accompanied Kate's copy of the manuscript that Ellie sent me, she told me that for some time she'd been hearing rumors about her property that almost amounted to an urban legend.

Apparently, during the long negotiations with the state of New York over the disposition of Kate's will and the settlement of property rights, Ellie had been made aware that there were squatters living in some of the buildings on the property.

By the time Ellie took possession, these squatters, mostly mentally ill and homeless people, had already been dispersed by state troopers. But she told me she'd found various possessions left behind.

Among them was a curious piece of artwork that seemed sufficiently interesting to her to hold onto. She sent me a scan of this drawing and I reproduce it here. As you can see, it seems to be some kind of nativity scene, except all but one of the participants seem to be beavers! The one human figure in it resembles pictures of Varnay which she also sent me.

The initial reason Ellie kept the picture was because it seemed interesting in the light of the urban legend that originated, as near as anyone could determine, from the squatters that had been living on her property.

Basically, the story was that there had been a rather advanced colony of beavers on her property and that a wizened, ancient-looking man lived with them, in what amounted to one of the most elaborate beaver communities ever seen; it was almost like a bustling beaver city.

She hadn't given these stories too much thought until after she read Kate's story. It, and some pictures of Charles Varnay that she'd seen, aroused her curiosity. When she decided to investigate, she found that an elaborate beaver colony had indeed mostly been on the portion of land that the state of New York had purchased from her.

Some photos had been taken of the land before it was cleared, and there had been some outcry from various animal rights groups over the

unseemly haste in which the clearing occurred.

HOTEL
When Ellie actually managed to confront some of the individuals involved, she was told that nothing inhumane occurred
because not only was no mysterious old man found there, but it was also claimed that not a single beaver was found there either.
The End